W9-AUS-422

iPod
The Missing Manual

Fifth Edition

iPod: The Missing Manual, Fifth Edition   BY J.D. BIERSDORFER

Copyright © 2007. All rights reserved.
Printed in Canada.

Published by O'Reilly Media, Inc., 1005 Gravenstein Highway North, Sebastopol, CA 95472.

O'Reilly books may be purchased for educational, business, or sales promotional use. Online editions are also available for most titles (*safari.oreilly.com*). For more information, contact our corporate/institutional sales department: 800.998.9938 or corporate@*oreilly.com*.

Executive Editor: Laurie Petrycki

Editor: Peter Meyers

Production Editor: Philip Dangler

Proofreader: Michele Filshie

Indexer: Dawn Mann

Cover Designers: Randy Comer, Karen Montgomery, and Suzy Wiviott

Interior Designer: Ron Bilodeau

Print History:
            November 2006:   First Edition.

ISBN-10: 0-596-52978-3
ISBN-13: 978-0-596-52978-9
[F]

Contents

The Missing Credits   ix
Introduction xiii

Chapter 1
Meet the iPod: Out of the Box and into Your Ears in 15 Minutes.   1
    Meet the iPod.   2
    Meet the iPod Nano   4
    Meet the iPod Shuffle   5
    Installing iTunes   6
    Unpacking and Connecting the iPod   7
    Three Ways to Get Music for iTunes (and iPod)   8
    Adding Music to the iPod Automatically. 10
    Adding Music to the iPod Manually 11
    Disconnecting the iPod from Your Computer 12
    Charging Your iPod the First Time 13
    Controlling Your iPod with the Click Wheel 14
    Other iPod Ports and Switches 15
    Finding the Music on Your iPod—and Playing It. 16

Chapter 2
Bopping Around the iPod 19
    Turning the iPod On and Off—or Putting It On Hold. 20
    Navigating the iPod's Menus. 21
    What's in the Music Menu 22
    What's in the Photos Menu. 23
    What's in the Videos Menu 24
    What's in the Extras Menu 25
    What's in the Settings Menu 26
    Two Other iPod Menu Items 28
    Some Idiot Set the iPod Menus to Greek. 29
    Customizing Your iPod's Menus. 30
    Setting Your iPod's Clock(s) 31
    Using Your iPod as an Alarm Clock. 32
    Letting Your iPod Put You to Sleep 33
    Searching for Songs on the iPod 34
    Jumping Around in Songs and Videos 35
    Adjusting the iPod's Volume 36
    Adjusting the Backlight Timer 37

How to Keep Your iPod Looking New. 38
Playing Games on an iPod 39
Reading the iPod Battery Meter. 41
Charging Your iPod Without the Computer 42
Locking Up Your Pod 43

Chapter 3
In Tune with iTunes **45**

The iTunes Window: An Introduction 46
Changing the Look of the iTunes Window. 48
Changing the Size of the iTunes Window 49
The iTunes Visualizer 50
Picking the Songs You Want to Rip. 51
Changing Import Settings for Better Audio Quality. 53
Three Ways to Browse Your Collection 54
Finding Your Songs in iTunes 55
Shuffling Your Music…and Smart Shuffle 56
You're the Critic: Rating Your Songs 57
Listening to Internet Radio 58
Sharing Your Music 59
Changing a Song's File Format 60
Evening Out Your Song Volumes 61
Improving Your Tunes with the Graphic Equalizer. 62
Finding (and getting rid of) Duplicate Songs. 64
Changing a Song's Start and Stop Times 65
Editing Song Information. 66
Editing Album Information. 67
Adding Artwork Automatically 68
Adding Artwork Manually. 69
Finding and Adding Lyrics to Your Song Files. 70
Viewing Artwork and Lyrics on the iPod 71
What iTunes Can Tell You About Your iPod. 72
Using iTunes to See What's on Your iPod. 73
Adjusting Your iPod's Preferences with iTunes 74
Loading Songs on an iPod from More Than One Computer 76
Manually Deleting Music and Videos from Your iPod. 77
Automatically Loading Your iPod Shuffle. 78
Manually Adding Music to the iPod Shuffle 79
Where iTunes Stores Your Files. 80
Moving Your iTunes Music Folder. 81
Backing Up Your iTunes Files. 82

Chapter 4

The Power of Playlists 85

Making a New Playlist 86
Changing an Existing Playlist. 88
Adding a Playlist to Your iPod 89
Making an On-The-Go Playlist 90
Deleting a Playlist 91
Party Shuffle: When You Want to Play DJ 92
Smart Playlists: Let iTunes Assemble Your Playlists. 93
Making Playlist Folders. 95
Three Kinds of Discs You Can Burn with iTunes. 96
Burning a Playlist to a CD 97
Printing Playlists and Snazzy CD Covers 98

Chapter 5

Shop the iTunes Store 101

Getting to the iTunes Store. 102
An Overview of the Store's Layout 103
Navigating the Aisles of the iTunes Store. 104
Setting Up an iTunes Store Account 105
Changing the Information in Your Apple Account 107
Tips for Dial-Up Music Lovers 108
Finding Music by Genre 109
Buying a Song or Album 110
Buying Movies or Videos 111
Buying Audio Books 112
Buying iPod Games 113
Downloading and Subscribing to Podcasts. 114
Usage Rights: What You Can Do with Your Purchases 115
Publishing Your Own Playlists (iMixes) 116
Other Cool iTunes Store Features. 117
iTunes Gift Certificates: Buying 'Em and Spending 'Em 118
Other Ways to Send iTunes Gifts 120
Using iTunes Allowance Accounts 121
Making an iTunes Wish List. 122
What to Do If Your Download Gets Interrupted 123
The Purchased Playlist 124
Setting Up Parental Controls for the Store. 125
Authorizing Your Computer for iTunes Purchases. 126
Deauthorizing Your Computer 128
Using Your iPod to Copy Purchases to Other Computers 129
Seeing Your iTunes Purchase History and Getting iTunes Store Help . . . 130

Chapter 6

Videos Everywhere. **133**

Adding Videos to iTunes. 134
Playing Videos in iTunes 135
Transferring Videos to the iPod 136
Playing Videos on the iPod 137
Video Formats That Work on the iPod 139
Finding iPod-Friendly Videos Online. 140
Video-Conversion Programs for the iPod. 142
Converting Your Own Home Movies 144
Converting Movie Files with iTunes 145
Playing iTunes and iPod Videos on Your TV 146
Burning Your Video Collection to DVD 148

Chapter 7

Picturing Your Photos on the iPod **151**

What You Need to Put Photos on Your iPod. 152
Getting Pictures onto the iPod 154
Digital Photographer Alert: Storing Full-Quality Photos on the iPod 156
Viewing Pictures on the iPod. 157
Playing Slideshows on the iPod 158
Playing Slideshows on a TV. 160

Chapter 8

Other Stuff the iPodCan Do for You **163**

Using Your iPod as an Address Book. 164
Using Your iPod as a Calendar 166
Tracking Time: Your iPod as a Stopwatch. 168
Tick-Tock: Your iPod as a World Clock 170
Using Your iPod as a Portable Hard Drive. 172
Reading Text Files on Your iPod 174
Recording Audio with Your iPod 176

Chapter 9

iPod Out Loud **179**

Checklist: Taking Your iPod on the Road 180
The FM Connection: Playing Your iPod Through a Radio's Speakers 182
Connecting Your iPod to a Car's Cassette Player 184
iPod and Serious Car Audio Fans: The Custom Installation 186
Finding a Power Source for Your iPod 188
Connecting the iPod to a Home Entertainment System 189
Streaming iTunes Music with the AirPort Express 191
Playing the iPod Through Portable Speakers 193
Where to Find Cool iPod Stuff. 195

Chapter 10

What to Do When the iPod Isn't Working Right. 199

Apple's Alphabet: The 5 Rs of iPod Repair 200

Resetting Your iPod 201

Downloading and Reinstalling iTunes and iTunes Updates 202

Using the Diagnostics Tools in iTunes for Windows. 203

Updating Your iPod's Software 204

Starting Over: Restoring Your iPod's Software. 206

Understanding the iPod's Battery Messages 208

Apple's Tips for Longer iPod Battery Life 209

Replacing Your iPod's Battery 210

AppleCare—What It Is and Whether You Need It 211

Finding an iPod Repair Shop. 212

Where to Find Apple's iPod Tutorials, Demos, and Help 213

Chapter 11

Advanced iPodding 217

Cool Software for Even More iPod Fun 218

Runners Alert: Use Your iPod Nano to Track Your Progress 219

Finding Alternative Headphones for Your iPod. 220

Getting Ideas for Playlists 221

What You Need to Make Your Own Podcast. 223

Recording Your Podcast 224

Publishing Your Podcast to Your Web Site or Blog. 225

Publishing your GarageBand Podcast to iWeb or the Web 226

Getting the iTunes Store to List Your Podcast. 227

Where to Get the Latest iPod News 228

Index. 231

The Missing Credits

About the Author

J.D. Biersdorfer is co-author of both *The Internet: The Missing Manual* and the second edition of *Google: The Missing Manual*. She's been writing the weekly computer Q&A column for *The New York Times* since 1998 and has covered everything from 17th-century Indian art to the world of female hackers for the newspaper. She's also written articles for the *AIGA Journal of Graphic Design* and *Rolling Stone* and has contributed essays about the collision of art and technology to several graphic-design books published by Allworth Press. She studied in the Theater & Drama program at Indiana University and now spends her limited spare moments playing the banjo and watching BBC World News. Email: jd.biersdorfer@gmail.com.

About the Creative Team

Peter Meyers (editor) works as an editor at O'Reilly Media on the Missing Manual series. He lives with his wife and cats in New York City. Email: *peter.meyers@gmail.com.*

Michele Filshie (copy editor) is O'Reilly's assistant editor for Missing Manuals and editor of four Personal Trainers (another O'Reilly series). Before turning to the world of computer-related books, Michele spent many happy years at Black Sparrow Press. She lives in Sebastopol and loves to get involved in local politics. Email: *mfilshie@oreilly.com.*

Dawn Mann (indexer) has been with O'Reilly for over three years and is currently an editorial assistant. When not working, she likes rock climbing, playing soccer, and generally getting into trouble. Email: *dawn@oreilly.com.*

Acknowledgements

I would like to thank David Pogue for suggesting this book to me way back in 2002, and then being a terrific editor through the mad scramble of the first two editions, and Peter Meyers, Chris Stone, and the Missing Manual folks at O'Reilly for guiding me through the past three updates. Thanks to Apple for courteously providing the iPod images and the assorted other iPod accessory companies who made their digital photography available. I'd also to thank all my friends and family (especially Betsy) for putting up with me every time Apple announces new iPod models and I disappear into my computer for several weeks.

The Missing Manual Series

Missing Manuals are witty, superbly written guides to computer products that don't come with printed manuals (which is just about all of them). Each book features a handcrafted index and RepKover, a detached-spine binding that lets the book lie perfectly flat without the assistance of weights or cinder blocks.

Recent and upcoming titles include:

Access 2007: The Missing Manual by Matthew MacDonald

Access 2007 for Starters: The Missing Manual by Matthew MacDonald

AppleScript: The Missing Manual by Adam Goldstein

Creating Web Sites: The Missing Manual by Matthew MacDonald

CSS: The Missing Manual by David Sawyer McFarland

Digital Photography: The Missing Manual by Chris Grover and Barbara Brundage

Dreamweaver 8: The Missing Manual by David Sawyer McFarland

eBay: The Missing Manual by Nancy Conner

Excel: The Missing Manual by Matthew MacDonald

Excel 2007: The Missing Manual by Matthew MacDonald

Excel 2007 for Starters: The Missing Manual by Matthew MacDonald

FileMaker Pro 8: The Missing Manual by Geoff Coffey and Susan Prosser

Flash 8: The Missing Manual by Emily Moore

FrontPage 2003: The Missing Manual by Jessica Mantaro

Google: The Missing Manual, 2nd Edition by Sarah Milstein, J.D. Biersdorfer, and Matthew MacDonald

iMovie HD 6: The Missing Manual by David Pogue

iPhoto 6: The Missing Manual by David Pogue

Mac OS X: The Missing Manual, Tiger Edition by David Pogue

Office 2004 for Macintosh: The Missing Manual by Mark H. Walker and Franklin Tessler

PCs: The Missing Manual by Andy Rathbone

PowerPoint 2007: The Missing Manual by Emily Moore

PowerPoint 2007 for Starters: The Missing Manual by Emily Moore

Quicken for Starters: The Missing Manual by Bonnie Biafore

Switching to the Mac: The Missing Manual, Tiger Edition by David Pogue and Adam Goldstein

The Internet: The Missing Manual by David Pogue and J.D. Biersdorfer

Windows 2000 Pro: The Missing Manual by Sharon Crawford

Windows XP for Starters: The Missing Manual by David Pogue

Windows XP Home Edition: The Missing Manual, 2nd Edition by David Pogue

Windows XP Pro: The Missing Manual, 2nd Edition by David Pogue, Craig Zacker, and Linda Zacker

Windows Vista: The Missing Manual by David Pogue

Windows Vista for Starters: The Missing Manual by David Pogue

Word 2007: The Missing Manual by Chris Grover

Word 2007 for Starters: The Missing Manual by Chris Grover

Introduction

Like the arrival of the Sony Walkman, which revolutionized the personal listening experience, Apple's introduction of the iPod in the fall of 2001 caught the world's ear. "With iPod, listening to music will never be the same again," intoned Steve Jobs, Apple's CEO. But even outside the Hyperbolic Chamber, the iPod was different enough to get attention. People noticed it, and more importantly, bought it.

If you're reading this book, odds are you're one of these folks. Or maybe you've just upgraded to a new iPod (or iPod Nano or iPod Shuffle) and want to learn about all the new features. In any case, welcome aboard!

With today's iPods, you can watch Hollywood feature films and TV shows, play popular video games, display gorgeous full-color photos, and look up personal phone numbers. You can quickly find out how to do all of that within these pages—and also learn everything you need to know about iTunes, the iPod's desktop software companion.

Only the full-sized iPod can play video, but all models still crank out the music— including the tiny clip-on iPod Shuffle, the loudest lapel pin on the market. Apple's mid-range model, the sporty iPod Nano, has its own small color screen to display personal photos, games, and album artwork.

But no matter which iPod you have, it's time to load it up with the music and other stuff that's important to you. Even the smallest model can hold hundreds of songs and play the Soundtrack of Your Life in any order you'd like.

Steve Jobs was right about the iPod. Things just haven't been the same since.

How to Use This Book

The tiny pamphlet that Apple includes in each iPod package is enough to get your iPod up and running, charged, and ready to download music.

But if you want to know more about how the iPod works, all the great things it can do, and where to find its secret features, the official pamphlet is skimpy in the extreme. And the iTunes help files that you have to read on your computer screen aren't much better: You can't mark your place or underline anything, there aren't any pictures or jokes, and you can't read them in the bathroom without fear of electrocution. This book lets you do all that, gives you more iPod info than the wee brochure, *and* it has nice color pictures.

About→These→Arrows

Throughout this book, and throughout the Missing Manual series, you'll find sentences like this one: "Open the View→Show Equalizer" menu. That's short-hand for a longer series of instructions that go something like:"Go to the menu bar in iTunes, click the View menu, and then select the Show Equalizer entry." Our shorthand system helps keep things much more snappy than those long, drawn out instructions.

The Very Basics

To use this book, and indeed to use a computer, you need to know a few basics. This book assumes that you're familiar with a few terms and concepts:

- **Clicking.** To *click* means to point the arrow cursor at something on the screen and then to press and release the clicker button on the mouse (or laptop trackpad). To *double-click*, of course, means to click twice in rapid succession, again without moving the cursor at all. To *drag* means to move the cursor *while* pressing the button.

When you're told to *Ctrl+click* something on a PC, or ⌘*-click* something on the Mac, you click while pressing the Ctrl or ⌘ key (both of which are near the Space bar).

- **Menus.** The *menus* are the words at the top of your screen or window: File, Edit, and so on. Click one to make a list of commands appear, as though they're written on a window shade you've just pulled down.

- **Keyboard shortcuts.** Jumping up to menus in iTunes *takes* time. Many keyboard quickies that perform the same menu functions are sprinkled throughout the book—Windows shortcuts first followed by Mac shortcuts in parentheses, just like this: "To quickly summon the Preferences box press Ctrl+comma (⌘-comma)."

If you've mastered this much information, you have all the technical background you need to enjoy *iPod: The Missing Manual*.

About MissingManuals.com

At the Web site, click the "Missing CD" link to reveal a neat, organized, chapter-by-chapter list of the shareware and freeware mentioned in this book. The Web site also offers corrections and updates to the book (to see them, click the book's title, then click Errata). In fact, you're invited and encouraged to submit such corrections and updates yourself. In an effort to keep the book as up to date and accurate as possible, each time we print more copies of this book, we'll make any confirmed corrections you've suggested. We'll also note such changes on the Web site, so that you can mark important corrections in your own copy of the book, if you like. And we'll keep the book current as Apple releases more iPods and software updates.

Safari® Enabled

When you see a Safari® Enabled icon on the cover of your favorite technology book that means the book is available online through the O'Reilly Network Safari Bookshelf.

Safari offers a solution that's better than e-books. It's a virtual library that lets you easily search thousands of top tech books, cut and paste code samples, download chapters, and find quick answers when you need the most accurate, current information. Try it for free at **http://safari.oreilly.com**.

1

Meet the iPod: Out of the Box and into Your Ears in 15 Minutes

I f you're like most people, you don't want to waste time getting your spiffy new iPod up and running. You probably don't want to wade through anything longer than a couple of paragraphs. Oh, and you'd like some color pictures, too.

Sure, Apple thoughtfully tucks a little pamphlet of starter info in with every iPod it sells. It's nicely designed as far as pamphlets go. But you may find that it doesn't go far enough. You want more help than a few line drawings and some haiku-like instructions.

This book—especially this chapter—can help you out.

You won't get bogged down in oceans of print here. You'll learn a bit about your iPod and how to get it whistling sweet tunes in your ear in a minimal amount of time. If you want more information on in-depth iPodding or getting the most out of iTunes, you can find that stuff in chapters farther down the road.

But for now, it's time to get rolling with your new iPod. Ready?

Meet the iPod

In just a few short years, Apple has transformed the iPod from a humble little 5-gigabyte music player with a black-and-white screen into a full color, gorgeous portable media system that can play movies, TV shows, and video games—all while still fitting comfortably in the palm of your hand. And it's come a long way from those first 5 gigabytes: now you can stuff 80 gigabytes of music, photos, videos, and more onto the biggest iPod.

In those 80 gigabytes, you can fit 20,000 songs or 100 hours of video. And you don't have to stock up on the Duracells, either, because the iPod's rechargeable battery can play audio for 20 hours or last for 6.5 hours if you're glued to your video library.

But if 80 gigabytes is too much for your needs, you can get the 30 GB model that does everything the big Podzilla model does, but just has a smaller hard drive. You can still store up to 7,500 songs or 40 hours of video on the device, which is plenty for many people. Battery life can last up to 14 hours for audio and 3.5 hours for video.

Both iPod models come in either black or white. If you're a diehard fan of a particular Irish rock band, you can also get the black 30 GB U2 Special Edition iPod with a sassy red click wheel front and center.

Along with the click wheel—think of it as the iPod's mouse—the 2.5-inch color screen is the player's other main element. Capable of displaying more than 65,000 colors at a resolution of 320 by 240 pixels (translation: high-quality), the iPod's a great place to store and show off your latest vacation photos, catch up on that episode of *The Daily Show* you missed, or play a few rounds of solitaire while listening to your favorite music.

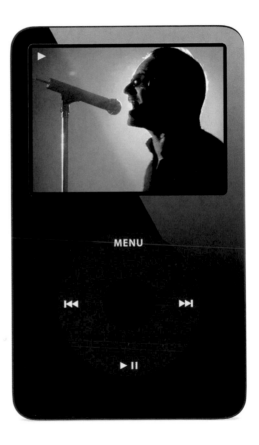

The iPod comes with everything you need to hook it up to your Windows PC or Macintosh: USB 2.0 cable, earphones, and even a slim case to keep the scuff monster at bay. Once you get up and iPodding around, you'll find that everyone and their grandmother wants to sell you other accessories for your iPod—all you have to do is stroll down to your favorite computer store and browse the offerings of fancy cases, cables, battery chargers, and more.

Meet the iPod Nano

The iPod Nano is Apple's mid-sized music player, but it doesn't just look like a regular iPod that got shrunk in the wash. The Nano has its own sleek, stylish design that brings a touch of fashion to your music experience. Like the big iPod, the Nano has a color screen and it plays songs, podcasts, and audio books. It can also display photos, text notes, contacts, and calendars. You navigate through all these goodies using the smooth, touch-sensitive click wheel.

There are, however, a few key differences between Nanos and regular iPods: you can't play videos or iTunes Store games like Pac-Man on it. But the Nano's great for workouts because it uses a flash memory chip to store music and photos. That means it's much more tolerant of jumping and flying around than a regular iPod, with its big ol' hard drive tucked inside.

The Nano comes in three sizes: 2-gigabyte, 4-gigabyte, and 8-gigabyte, all wrapped in sturdy, scratch-resistant anodized aluminum. You're not just stuck with a black-or-white decision when buying a Nano, either—you can get the 4 GB model in silver, green, blue, or pink. Oh, and if you like your music flowing all day long, you'll be glad to know the Nano's battery lasts up to 24 hours—you'll probably conk out before it does.

Meet the iPod Shuffle

The latest version of the iPod Shuffle is even smaller than the original white-stick edition. And you don't have to worry about losing the new silver Shuffle, because it clips right to your lapel or pocket—it's like jewelry you can rock out with. Like the first Shuffle, this iPod doesn't have a screen, and its 1-gigabyte memory chip holds about 240 songs. And just because it's called the iPod Shuffle, doesn't mean you have to shuffle your music; you can play your songs (or audio books) in order with the nudge of a button.

This silver surfer is so small, it doesn't even have room for the USB jack that its predecessor used to plug into the computer for music-loading and battery-recharging. The new Shuffles, which offer about 12 hours of playing time, now include a tiny dock that connects the player to your computer's USB port. In addition to the dock, you also get:

❶ Those trademark white Apple headphones, all ready to plug into the headphone jack on the top of the Shuffle.

❷ A handy control ring on the front of the player to adjust your volume and skip over songs you're not in the mood to hear.

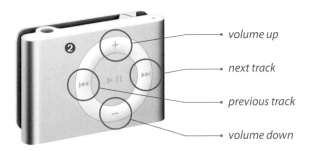

- *volume up*
- *next track*
- *previous track*
- *volume down*

❸ Little silver switches on bottom of the Shuffle to turn it off and on and to flip between shuffling your songs and playing them in order.

Installing iTunes

Before you can have hours of iPod fun, you need to install the iTunes program on your computer. With iTunes, you also get Apple's QuickTime multimedia software—a video helper for iTunes. iPods once came with a CD packing all this software, but these days you have to download it yourself:

❶ **Fire up your Web browser and point it to** *http://www.apple.com/ipod/start.*

❷ **Click the "Download iTunes" button.** (Turn off the "Email me..." and "Keep me up to date..." checkboxes to spare yourself future marketing missives.) Wait for the file to download to your computer.

❸ **When the file lands on your hard drive, double-click the** *iTunesSetup.exe* **file.** If you use a Mac, double-click the *iTunes.dmg* file and then open the *iTunes.mpkg* file to start the installation. But if your Mac's younger than five years old, you probably already have iTunes installed. Go to Menu→Software Update and ask your Mac to look for a newer version just in case.

❹ **Follow the screens until the software installer says it's done.**

You may need to restart your computer after the software's been installed. Once iTunes is loaded, you're ready to connect your new iPod to the computer.

Unpacking and Connecting the iPod

If you haven't torn open the package already, carefully take the iPod out of its box. The items you'll find inside vary depending on which iPod you purchased, but all of them come with:

❶ The classic Apple white headphones.

❷ A USB cable to connect the iPod to your computer. The iPod and iPod Nano use the same white USB cable with the flat dock-connector port, while the iPod Shuffle has its own little USB dock.

❸ A little pamphlet of basic quick-start information that's not nearly as fun or as colorful as this book.

What you want right now is the USB cable. Connect the small end to the computer's USB port and the large, flat end (or the dock, if you have a Shuffle) to the iPod. The first time you connect the iPod to the computer, the Setup Assistant walks you through a few steps to get your iPod ready to go.

The next step, if you want to hear some music, is to *get* some music on your iPod.

Three Ways to Get Music for iTunes (and iPod)

Once iTunes is installed on your computer, you can start filling it with music. Chapter 3 has info on digital audio formats and technical settings you can tweak, but if you've got a brand new iPod, odds are you don't care about *that* right now. No, you'd probably just like to get some music on your iPod. Here are three simple ways:

Letting iTunes find existing songs

If you've had a computer for longer than a few years, odds are you already have some songs in the popular MP3 format already on your hard drive. When you start iTunes for the first time, the program asks if you'd like it to search your PC or Mac for music and add it to iTunes. Click "Yes" and iTunes will go fetch.

 Now, many Windows fans, if they do have existing music, may have songs in the Windows Media Audio (WMA) format. The bad news here is that iTunes can't play WMA files. The good news is that iTunes, when it finds WMA files, can automatically convert them to an iPod-friendly format.

Converting music from a CD

You can also use iTunes to convert tracks from your audio CDs into iPod-ready digital music files. Just stick a CD in your computer's disc drive after you start up iTunes. The program asks if you want to import the CD into iTunes. (If it doesn't, just click the "Import CD" button at the bottom of the iTunes window.)

Once you tell it to import the music, iTunes gets to work. If you're connected to the Internet, the program automatically downloads song titles and artist information for the CD and begins to add the songs to the iTunes library. You can import all the tracks from a CD, but if you don't want every song, then turn off the checkbox next to those titles and iTunes skips them. Chapter 3 has more about using iTunes to convert CDs.

Buying music in the iTunes Store

Another way to get music for iPod and iTunes is to buy it from the iTunes Store. Click the iTunes Store icon in the list on the left side of iTunes. Once you land on the Store's main page and set up your iTunes account, you can buy and download songs, audio books, and videos. The content goes straight into your iTunes library and then onto your iPod. Chapter 5 is all about using the iTunes Store.

Adding Music to the iPod Automatically

You don't have to do much to keep your music and video collection up to date between your computer and your iPod. That's because the iPod has a nifty *autosync* feature, which automatically synchronizes your iTunes library to the iPod when you connect it to the computer.

The first time you plug in your new iPod (after you've installed iTunes, of course), the iPod Setup Assistant leaps into action, asks you to name your iPod, and asks if you'd like to "Automatically sync songs and videos to my iPod" right there. If your answer's "yes," just click the Finish button. iTunes loads a copy of everything in its library onto your iPod. That's it. Your iPod's ready to go.

If you like autosync but want more control over what goes onto the iPod, check out Chapter 3.

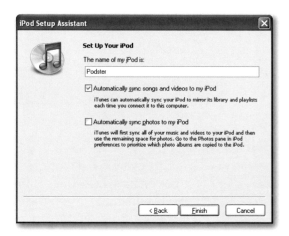

 Note If you have an iPod Shuffle, you may already have more music than can fit on the small player. If that's the case, *your* automatic option is the Autofill button at the bottom of the iTunes window. Click that and iTunes decides what to put on your iPod. If you want to be the boss of your music, read the next page.

Adding Music to the iPod Manually

If you don't have enough room on your iPod for your whole iTunes collection, or plan to load music onto your iPod from more than one computer, (say your work and home PCs), you'll want to *manually manage* your songs and other stuff. To put your iPod on manual right from the get-go turn off the checkbox on the iPod Setup Assistant screen next to "Automatically sync songs..." (If you've already done the Setup Thing, see Chapter 3 for how to come back to Manual Land.) iTunes now refrains from automatically dumping everything onto your iPod. "But," you ask, "*How* do I get the music on there by myself?" It's easy. You just drag it:

❶ **In iTunes, click the Music icon under Library.** All your song titles appear in the main window. Click the eyeball-shaped icon (down at the bottom) to reveal your collection grouped by Artist or Album.

❷ **Click the album name or song titles you want to copy to the iPod.** Grab multiple song titles or albums by holding down the Control (⌘) key.

❸ **Drag your selection onto the iPod icon.** The number of songs you're dragging appears inside a red circle.

You can manually place any items in your iTunes library—audio books, movies, whatever—onto your iPod this way.

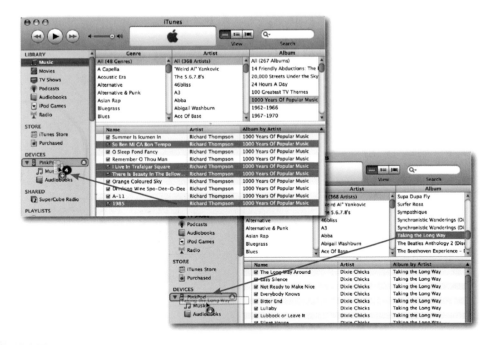

Disconnecting the iPod from Your Computer

Got iTunes installed? *Check.*

Got music in the iTunes library? *Check.*

Got the iPod connected and the music you want copied onto it? *Check.*

Next up: disconnect the iPod from your computer so you can enjoy your tunes. Resist the impulse to yank the USB cable out of the iPod without checking the iPod's screen first. If you see a big "Do Not Disconnect" sign on the screen, don't unplug just yet. (If the iPod's showing its menus or the battery charging icon, then you can safely unplug it.)

If you see the red Disconnect warning or you've opted to manually manage your iPod (as explained on the previous page), you need to *manually* eject the iPod from your computer. iTunes gives you two easy ways to do this:

❶ Click the little Eject icon next to the name of your iPod in the iTunes Source list.

❷ If your iPod's already selected in the Source list, click the Eject iPod button down on the bottom-right corner of iTunes.

With either method, once the "Do Not Disconnect" screen goes away, you can safely liberate your iPod.

Charging Your iPod the First Time

Right out of the box, your iPod's battery probably has enough juice to run for a little while without having to charge it up. When it comes time to charge the battery, all you need to do is plug the iPod back into your computer with the USB cable (the iPod charges itself by drawing from your Mac or PC's power). Just make sure the computer is turned on and isn't asleep.

It takes only a few hours to fully charge your iPod's battery, and even less time to do what Apple calls a *fast charge*, which fills up 80 percent of the battery's capacity. That should be plenty of gas in your iPod's tank for a quick spin.

Here's how much time each type of iPod needs for both a fast charge and a full charge:

	Fast Charge	Full Charge
iPod	2 hours	4 hours
iPod Nano	1.5 hours	3 hours
iPod Shuffle	2 hours	4 hours

If you're traveling and don't want to drag your laptop with you just to charge your iPod, you can buy an AC adapter for it. Chapter 2 has more information on that.

Controlling Your iPod with the Click Wheel

Smack in the iPod's belly is the click wheel, your way around the iPod's contents. It's called a click wheel because you can actually click down on the four buttons evenly arranged around the ring. The menus onscreen spin by as your thumb moves around the circle. There's also a big button in the wheel's center, which you'll be pushing a lot as you use your iPod. Here's what each button does, going clockwise from the top.

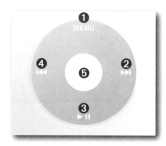

❶ **Menu.** Tap this button to return to any screen you've just viewed. For example, if you've visited Music→Playlists→My Top Rated, then press Menu twice to return to the Music menu. If you keep tapping Menu, you eventually wind up on the main iPod menu.

❷ **Fast-forward/Next.** Press this button to jump to the next song in a playlist (Chapter 4), or hold it down to advance quickly within a song.

❸ **Play/Pause.** Like on a CD player, this button starts a song; push it again to pause the music.

❹ **Rewind/Previous.** Press this button to play the song directly before the current track (or hold it down to "rewind" within a song).

❺ **Select.** Like clicking a mouse button, press Select to choose a highlighted menu item. When a song title's highlighted, the Select button also begins playback.

Other iPod Ports and Switches

On the outside, the iPod isn't a very complicated device. There's really just a Hold switch and two jacks to plug in cords. Here's what you do with each one.

❶ **Hold Switch.** At the top of the iPod, over on the left side, is a little sliding switch marked Hold. This is a control that deactivates all the iPod's front buttons. Turning on the Hold switch can stop your iPod from popping on if the buttons accidentally get bumped.

❷ **Headphone Jack.** Your new iPod comes with its own bright white headphones, and they plug in right here. If you don't like Apple's headphones, you can use another style or brand, as long as the other headphones use the standard 3.5-millimeter stereo miniplug.

❸ **Dock Connector.** The flat port on the iPod's bottom is called the Dock Connector. This is where you plug in the USB cable so you can connect iPod to computer for battery-charging and music- and video-fill ups.

Finding the Music on Your iPod— and Playing It

Now that you've got some songs on the iPod, you're ready to listen to them. Plug your headphones into the headphone jack and press any button on the front of the iPod if you need to turn it on.

 Note The first time you turn on your iPod, it asks you what language to use for the iPod menus. If you're reading this book, you probably want English, which is at the very top of the list.

After you pick a language, the first menu you see says iPod at the top of the screen. Here's how to start playing your tunes:

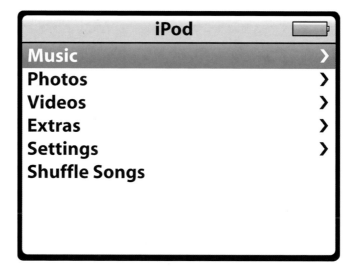

❶ **On the iPod menu, highlight the Music menu.** Run your thumb over the scroll wheel to move the blue highlight bar up and down.

❷ **Press the round center button to select Music.**

❸ **On the Music menu, scroll to whichever category you want to use to find your song.** Your choices include Artist, Album, Song, Genre, and so on. Scroll to the one you want and press the center button to see your songs sorted by your chosen method.

❹ **Scroll through the list on the iPod's screen.** Say you decided to look for music by Artist. You now see a list of all the singers and bands stored on your iPod. Scroll down to the one you want and press the center button. A list of all the albums you have from that artist appears on screen.

❺ **Scroll to the one you want to hear.** Press the Play/Pause button to start playing the album.

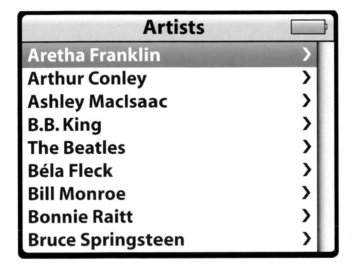

You can find anything on your iPod by scrolling around and pressing the center button to select the item you want to hear, watch, read or play. If you end up on a screen where you don't want to be, then press the Menu button to retrace your steps. In fact, you can keep pressing the Menu button to reverse course and go all the way back to the iPod's main menu.

Press the Play/Pause button to pause a song that's playing. If a song's not playing and you don't touch the iPod's buttons for a few minutes, it puts itself to sleep automatically to save battery power.

2

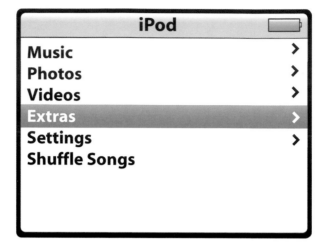

iPod	🔋
Music	›
Photos	›
Videos	›
Extras	›
Settings	›
Shuffle Songs	

Bopping Around the iPod

The iPod is a very simple device to operate—five buttons and a click wheel quickly take you to all your songs, movies, games, audio books, and everything else parked on your 'Pod. Even though it doesn't have a mouse, the player's controls work just like a desktop computer: you highlight an item onscreen and click the center button to select it.

Performing this action either takes you to another menu of options or starts a function—like playing a song, calling up your calendar, or checking the time in Paris. This chapter shows you what lies underneath all the menus on your iPod or iPod Nano and what each item does. Shuffle owners will find special coverage of their screenless wonders sprinkled throughout the chapter.

Turning the iPod On and Off— or Putting It On Hold

The iPod has only five buttons and one switch—and none of them are labeled Off or On. It's not hard to do either, even without official buttons.

- To turn the iPod on, just tap any button on the front and it wakes right up, ready to play music or movies.

- To turn the iPod off, press the Play/Pause button for a few seconds until the screen goes off. To preserve battery power, an inactive iPod automatically shuts itself off after a couple of minutes.

However, if its front buttons get bumped, say, in a purse or backpack, the iPod can turn on and run its battery down without you knowing it. Then you end up with a drained iPod right before that long commute home.

That's where the Hold switch on the top of the iPod comes in handy. Just slide it over so the orange bit underneath shows, and your iPod's front buttons are deactivated and won't respond to inadvertent taps. Flicking the Hold switch is good for preventing accidental battery drains; it's great if you have the iPod in your pocket and don't want to jump to the next song every time you inadvertently graze the click wheel.

Navigating the iPod's Menus

Like any modern computer program, the iPod's user interface is made up of a series of menus and sub-menus. The top-level, or main menu, just says iPod at the top of the screen. No matter how deeply you burrow into the player's submenus, you can always get back to the main iPod menu by pressing the menu button on the click wheel.

In fact, think of iPod navigation like this: Press the round center button to go deeper into the menus and press the Menu button to back out and retrace your steps.

The contents of your iPod menu varies a bit depending on which model you have—except for the Shuffle, which doesn't have a screen or menus. Here's the basic lineup:

- Music
- Photos
- Videos (full size iPod only)

- Extras
- Settings
- Shuffle Songs

The next few pages give you a little more information about each menu. And just as the iPod and iTunes give you choices about your music, you can also decide for yourself what you want displayed on your main menu. If you like the sound of that, check out "Customizing Your iPod's Menus" later in this chapter.

What's in the Music Menu

In the Music menu you'll find a one-stop shopping center for your iPod's audio-related options, including tunes, audio books, and podcasts.

- **Playlists.** A *playlist* is a customized list of songs you create. Chapter 4 has loads more info on creating playlists.

- **Artists.** This menu groups every tune by the performer's name.

- **Albums.** Your music, grouped by album.

- **Songs.** All the songs on your iPod, listed alphabetically.

- **Podcasts.** All your prerecorded radio-style programs.

- **Genres.** Your music, sorted by type: rock, rap, country, and so on.

- **Composers.** Your music, grouped by songwriter.

- **Audiobooks.** Your iPod's spoken-word content.

- **Search.** When you have a ton of tunes and don't feel like scrolling through your collection, use the Search function to scroll-and-click in the first few letters on a tiny onscreen keyboard. Songs that match pop up in their own list.

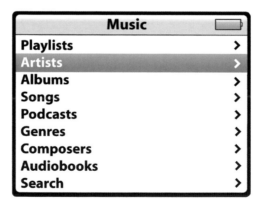

Even without using the Search function, the Music menu's sub-menus make it easy to find specific music. For example, to see a list of all songs on your iPod sorted by artist, select Artists from the Music menu. The next screen presents you with an alphabetical list of bands and singers.

What's in the Photos Menu

Turn your iPod into a pocket photo viewer. Once you stock your iPod with images (Chapter 7 has instructions), the Photos menu lets you adjust picture-viewing preferences—including slideshow settings for picture collections—and call up your actual pix. (The TV-related settings aren't available on the Nano.)

Slideshow Settings

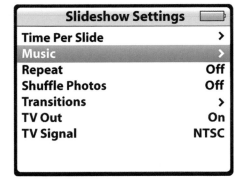

- **Time Per Slide.** Linger up to 20 seconds on each photo or manually click through each picture.

- **Music.** Select a playlist as your soundtrack, or choose silence.

- **Repeat.** As with playlists, slideshows can repeat—if you want 'em to.

- **Shuffle Photos.** Toggle the setting to On to randomly display each photo in a slideshow.

- **Transitions.** Options here include a classic Hollywood wipe, a dissolve, and many more.

- **TV Out.** To display your slideshow on a connected TV, select On or Ask. For slideshows on the iPod, choose Off or Ask. (Off does what it says; Ask nags you to pick between TV and iPod before the show starts.)

- **TV Signal.** When connected to a TV in North or South America, or East Asia, select NTSC; most other places use the PAL standard.

Photo Library

Click here to view your iPod's entire photo library; individual albums are listed below the Photo Library menu. Chapter 7 shows you how to summon your pictures onscreen.

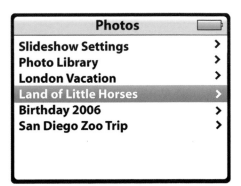

What's in the Videos Menu

That full-sized iPod is also a personal movie player. Before you grab the pop-corn, here's what you'll find on its menu of video-setting and sorting options:

- **Video Playlists.** Just like music, you can create playlists of videos in iTunes.

- **Movies.** Go here to find full-length feature films from the iTunes Store and your own home movies.

- **Music Videos.** A list of your collected music video clips.

- **TV Shows.** A menu for iTunes Store-purchased episodes and personally recorded shows.

- **Video Podcasts.** Some podcasts have pictures now; look here when they do.

- **Video Settings.** You can configure your TV playback options just like the TV Out and TV Signal choices listed on the previous page. You can also set the iPod to play video in widescreen format or adjust it for full-screen viewing.

Playing a video works just like playing a song: browse, scroll, and select. Chapters 5 and 6 tell you how to buy, sort, and organize your iPod's video collection from the iTunes side of the fence.

What's in the Extras Menu

Here lies all the goodies that make the iPod more than just a music player:

- **Clock.** With its built-in clock and ability to display multiple different time zones, the iPod is probably the most stylish pocket watch you'll ever see.

- **Games.** You can play the historic Brick game and you also get Parachute, Solitaire, and a Music Quiz. Games from the iTunes Store, like Tetris and Mahjong, also land here.

- **Contacts.** Any phone numbers and addresses you've ported over from your computer reside here.

- **Calendar.** This menu holds a copy of your personal daily schedule from iCal or Microsoft Outlook.

- **Notes.** The iPod has a built-in text reader program that you can use to read short documents and notes.

- **Stopwatch.** The iPod can serve as your timer for keeping track of your overall workout or multiple laps around the track.

- **Screen Lock.** With all your stuff that's nobody's business—address book, schedule, photos, etc.—you may want to password protect your 'Pod.

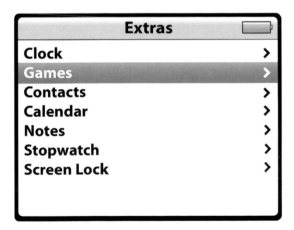

Check out Chapter 8 for more information on turning your iPod into a time-keeper, a handheld organizer, and more.

What's in the Settings Menu

The Settings menu has more than a dozen options for tailoring your iPod's look and sound.

- **About.** Look here for your iPod's name; the number of songs, videos, and photos on it; your model's hard drive capacity; and how much free disk space you have.

- **Main Menu.** Customize which items appear in your iPod's main menu here.

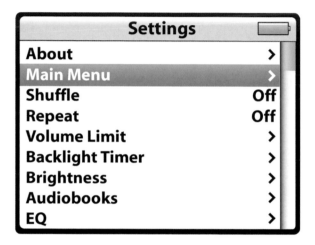

- **Shuffle.** Turn this feature on to shuffle songs or albums.

- **Repeat.** Repeat One plays the current song over and over; Repeat All repeats the current album, playlist or song library.

- **Volume Limit.** Keep your (or your child's) eardrums from melting by setting a maximum volume limit—and locking it.

- **Backlight Timer.** Specify how long the backlight stays on each time you press a button or turn the dial—from 1 Second to Always On.

- **Brightness.** If your iPod movies seem a bit dim (and not just because of Hollywood's standards), use this setting to brighten the screen.

- **Audiobooks.** This setting lets you speed up or slow down the narrator's voice.

- **EQ.** Apply more than 20 different equalizer presets for acoustic, classical, hip hop, and other types of music. Chapter 3 has more on equalization.

- **Compilations.** Turning this setting to On lets you add a Compilations submenu to the main Music menu so those hard-to-sort soundtracks, all-star albums and other group efforts show up as one album.

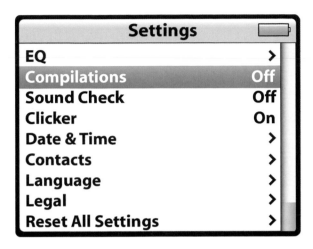

- **Sound Check.** Turning on Sound Check helps level out songs of differing volumes. Chapter 3 has more info.

- **Clicker.** Some people think the Clicker noise during a long scroll sounds like ants tap dancing. Others like the audio cue. Decide for yourself and turn the sound off or on here.

- **Date & Time.** Adjust your iPod's date, time, and time zone settings here.

- **Contacts.** This setting lets you change the sorting order of the first and last names of people in your iPod's address book.

- **Language.** The iPod can display its menus in most major European and Asian languages. Pick one here.

- **Legal.** The Legal menu contains a long scroll of copyright notices for Apple and its software partners. It's not very interesting reading unless perhaps you're studying intellectual-property law.

- **Reset All Settings.** This command returns all your iPod's customized sound and display settings back to their original factory settings.

Two Other iPod Menu Items

One—sometimes two—other items live down at the bottom of the iPod's main menu.

Shuffle Songs

The mystical, magical qualities of the iPod's Shuffle Songs setting (*"How does my little PeaPod always know when to play my Weird Al Yankovic and Monty Python songs to cheer me up?"*) have become one of the player's most popular features since the early days of iPodding. So Apple moved Shuffle out to the main menu. Just scroll and select if you want to shuffle your songs.

Now Playing

When you have a song playing—but have scrolled back to the main menu to do something else while jamming—the Now Playing item appears at the very bottom of the screen. Highlight this command and press Select to call up your song's Now Playing screen and get back to the music at hand.

Tip iPod Shuffle owners, this one's just for you: To jump back to the very first song on your Shuffle's playlist, flip the shuffle switch to Play In Order (which looks like two arrows chasing each other's tails). Then click the Play/Pause button three times fast.

Some Idiot Set the iPod Menus to Greek

Changing the iPod's onscreen language to an unfamiliar alphabet is a favorite trick of jealous co-workers and older brothers. Fortunately, you have a couple of ways to get the iPod back to English.

First, click the Menu button until you get back to the iPod's main menu screen. You'll see "iPod" in English at the top, and the menu listings in whatever language your wisenheimer pal picked out for you. Then follow these steps:

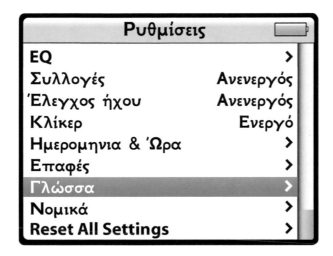

❶ **Scroll down to the fifth line on your iPod—or the fourth line if you have a Nano.** You've just highlighted the Settings menu; click it.

❷ **Select this item and scroll to "Reset All Settings," which conveniently appears in English.** Here, you can make a decision:

Option 1: The *third* menu item from the bottom is the Language setting. Scroll up there to get to the language list and then choose English.

Option 2: If you're tired of your iPod settings, you can wipe them out and start over. Click Reset All Settings. The next screen gives you a choice: Cancel or Reset.

❸ **Scroll down to the last entry: "Reset All Settings," (also in English) to get back to the Language menu, where you can select "English" for the iPod.**

Customizing Your iPod's Menus

The iPod has a handy personalization feature: the ability to arrange your iPod's Main Menu screen so that only the items you like show up there. For example, you could insert the Calendar option onto the iPod's opening screen so that you don't have to drill down through the Extras menu to get at it.

To customize your iPod's Main Menu, start by choosing Settings→Main Menu from the main iPod menu. You see a list of items that you can choose to add or eliminate from your iPod's main screen: Music, Playlists, Artists, Albums, and so on.

As you scroll down the list, press the Select button to turn each one on or off. You might, for example, consider adding these commands:

- **Clock,** for quick checks of the time.

- **Games,** for quick killing of time.

- **Contacts,** to look up phone numbers and call people to pass the time.

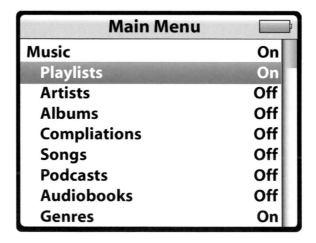

To see the fruits of your labor, press Menu twice to return to the main screen. Sure enough, in addition to the usual commands described in this chapter, you'll see the formerly buried commands right out front, ready to go.

Setting Your iPod's Clock(s)

When you choose Clock from the iPod's Extras menu, you can set up live clocks tracking multiple cities. This little timekeeper comes in handy if you forget your watch. To create a clock, choose Clock→New Clock and pick the location you want on the Region menu; then choose a city on the next screen. Each clock comes with its own submenus:

- **Alarm Clock.** Set up an audio alert—no headphones required—to wake you up.

- **Change City.** This menu takes you back to the Region menu when you need to relocate.

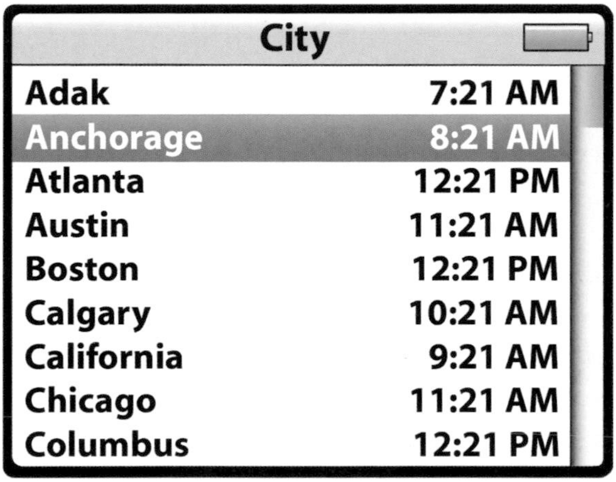

City	
Adak	**7:21 AM**
Anchorage	**8:21 AM**
Atlanta	**12:21 PM**
Austin	**11:21 AM**
Boston	**12:21 PM**
Calgary	**10:21 AM**
California	**9:21 AM**
Chicago	**11:21 AM**
Columbus	**12:21 PM**

- **Daylight Savings Time.** Press the Select button to turn Daylight Savings Time off or on.

- **Delete This Clock.** Get rid of any clock with one click.

- **Sleep Timer.** Just as the iPod can awaken you, it can send you off to Dreamland (with the music of your choice). The next page has more information on doing both.

> **Tip** You can ask iPod to display the current time in its title bar whenever music's playing. Just choose iPod→Settings→Date & Time→Time in Title. Press the Select button to toggle the "Time in Title" display on or off.

Using Your iPod as an Alarm Clock

The alarm clock can give you a gentle nudge when you need it. To set your iPod's alarm:

❶ **Choose Extras→Clock→[Location Name]→Alarm Clock→Alarm. Press the Select button.** The Alarm changes to On.

❷ **Scroll to Time, press Select.** On the Alarm Time screen, as you turn the wheel, you change the time the iPod displays in the highlighted box. Press the Select button as you pick the hour, minutes, and so on.

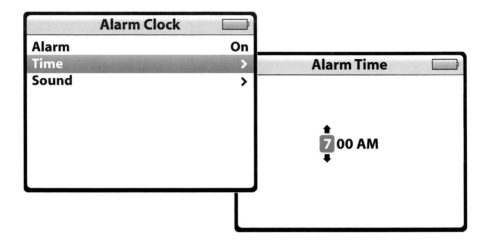

❸ **Press Select again to set the time.** It's time to decide whether you want "Beep" (a warbling R2-D2-like noise that comes out of the iPod's built-in speaker) or music. If you choose music, it plays through your headphones, assuming they haven't fallen out—or an external set of speakers if you have some.

❹ **Scroll to Sound and press Select. Choose Beep or highlight the playlist you want. Press Select.** The Alarm Clock's set (a bell appears on the main clock screen). When the alarm goes off, just press the iPod's Pause button to stop it.

If you wake up early and want to turn off the alarm, go to Extras→Clock Extras→ Alarm Clock Extras→Alarm and press the Select button to toggle it off.

Letting Your iPod Put You to Sleep

The iPod's sleep timer is like the opposite of the alarm clock: It's designed to help you fall *asleep* instead of waking you. The idea is that you can schedule the iPod to shut itself off after a specified period of time so you can doze off as music plays, without running down your battery.

To set the iPod's Sleep Timer, choose Extras→Clock→[Location Name]→Sleep Timer. Scroll down to the amount of time you want: 15, 20, 60, 90, or 120 minutes. (You can also choose to turn off the Sleep Timer here.)

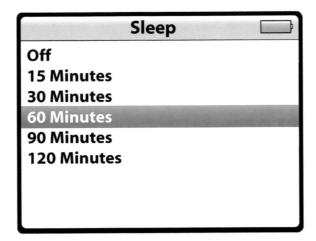

Now, start the iPod playing (press Play) and snuggle down into your easy chair or pillow. The screen displays a little clock and begins a digital countdown to sleepy-land.

Your iPod will stop playing automatically after the appointed interval—but if all goes well, you won't be awake to notice.

Searching for Songs on the iPod

As your music collection grows, scrolling to find a specific song or album can leave your thumb weary. Sometimes, you may not even remember if you *have* a certain song on the iPod. The Search feature, available on the second-generation versions of both the iPod Nano and the full-sized iPod, lets you drill down through your massive library and locate specific songs, albums, and so on with a few spins of the click wheel. It works like this:

❶ Choose iPod→Music→Search.

❷ On the screen that appears, use the click wheel to highlight a letter from the alphabet. Press the center button to select a letter.

❸ The iPod immediately presents a list of narrowed down matching titles, winnowing it further as you select more letters. Use the backspace key (the leftward arrow) to pluck out letters you don't want.

❹ Once the title you want appears onscreen, click Done.

The alphabet row goes away, but the song (or songs) stays front and center—and selectable.

Jumping Around in Songs and Videos

Sometimes, you just have to hear the good part again or watch that scene in the movie once more because it was so cool the first time. If that's the case, the iPod gives you the controls to do so.

Hold down the Rewind/Previous and the Fast-forward/Next buttons on either side of the click wheel to zip back and forth through the song or video clip.

If you want to get to a specific time in the song or video, press the iPod's center button and then use the wheel to scroll over to the exact spot in the track's onscreen timeline. For an audio file, a small diamond appears in the timeline when you press the center button so you can see where you are in the song.

This jump-to-the-best-part technique is called *scrubbing*, so if a fellow iPodder tells you to scrub over to 2:05 in the song to hear that great guitar solo, the person's not talking about cleaning.

Adjusting the iPod's Volume

The control ring on the iPod Shuffle has plus (+) and minus (-) buttons to pump up (or down) your music's volume. The volume knob on the larger iPods is virtual. With the song or video playing, run your thumb over the click wheel; the timeline bar on the bottom switches to a volume-level indicator.

If you want to protect your hearing, use the Volume Limit setting to lock in a maximum volume of your own choosing. Parents who worry that their kids are blasting music too loudly can set a Volume Limit and lock it with a numeric password:

❶ Go to iPod→Settings→Volume Limit.

❷ On the next screen, use the click wheel to select the highest volume level you want to have on the volume bar.

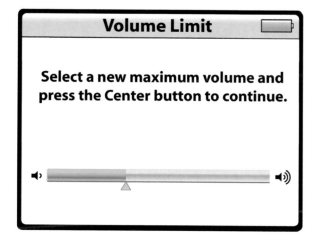

❸ Press the center button to move to the next screen.

❹ If you want to lock this setting, select Set Combination.

❺ The iPod's Screen Lock display appears and you can dial in a secret four-number password that must be entered again in order to change the setting.

Adjusting the Backlight Timer

That bright, white backlight on the iPod illuminates the screen nicely when you have to scroll around to find a song—and it also makes a great impromptu flashlight at night when you're fumbling around, trying to unlock the front door. The backlight, brilliant as it is, however, tends to be something of a battery hog and if you leave it on all the time, you'll notice a definite decrease in the amount of battery time you get between charges.

But some people do like the backlight to stay on for a tad longer than just those few default seconds. Fortunately, the iPod gives you an option for controlling how long the light appears. To dial up more or less light, go to iPod→ Settings→Backlight Timer. Here, you can pick increments from 2 to 20 seconds of iPod Illumination.

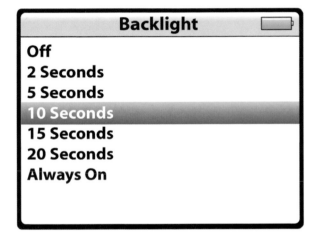

How to Keep Your iPod Looking New

New iPods have a shiny, glossy glow about them, but keeping the player looking pristine can be an effort, especially if it gets tossed into a backpack, shoved in a pocket, and generally hauled around town. The LCD screen is especially delicate.

XtremeMac's "TuffWrap" case for the iPod Nano.

A good case helps keep your iPod looking good and functioning well. Not only does a case shield the surface from the dings and scratches of daily life, a sturdy bit of additional armor can help protect the iPod's innards if it ever makes an accidental landing on a hard surface. You can find iPod cases for every taste and style online and off. You can find great cases at Everything iPod (*www.everythingipod.com*), XtremeMac (*www.xtrememac.com*), and the Think Different Store (*www.thinkdifferentstore.com*), to mention a few.

DLO's "Relaxed Leather" case for the iPod.

If you do have a scratched or smudged iPod, cleaning solutions like iKlear (*www.klearscreen.com*) and iCleaner (*www.ipodcleaner.com*) may help shine things up.

Playing Games on an iPod

The iPod is a personal entertainment machine on many levels. All current iPod and iPod Nano models have four games: Brick, Music Quiz, Parachute and—perhaps the most popular time-waster ever—Solitaire. If you have a full-sized iPod, you can also buy and download old-school video games like Pac-Man, Tetris, Texas Hold'Em, and more from the iPod Games area of the iTunes Store (Chapter 5). To find any of your games, go to iPod→Extras→Games.

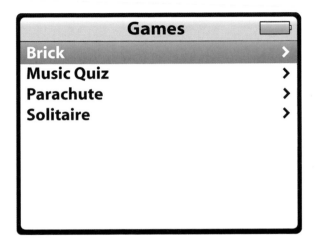

Brick

Your mission, should you choose to accept it, is to use a ricocheting ball to break through rows of bricks at the top of the screen. Press the Select button to start the game: As the small ball rockets in from the side, use the click wheel to move the paddle (at the bottom) in an effort to deflect the ball into the bricks above.

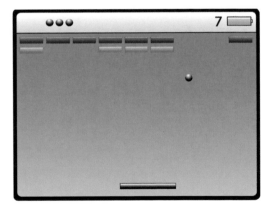

Music Quiz

The game plays the first few seconds of a random song from your library. You have 10 seconds to pick out the song's title from the 5 names listed on the screen. If you miss, you get a "Wrong" message onscreen and a deep sense of shame for not knowing your own music collection. Choosing the correct title adds to your running score and advances you to the next song.

Parachute

The iPod's Parachute game lets you assume control of a ground-based anti-aircraft gun. You're supposed to shoot at the helicopters that fly overhead and drop tiny little parachuting stick-people. The gun sits in the center bottom of the screen, but you can use the click wheel to pivot the barrel and direct your fire to the helicopters. Press the Select button to fire at either the helicopters or the tiny parachutists.

Solitaire

The iPod's version of the game is standard Klondike: You get a row of seven card piles, on which you're supposed to alternate black and red cards in descending numerical order. Use the click wheel to pass the hand over each stack of cards. When you get to the card you want, click the Select button to move the selected card to the bottom of the screen. Then scroll the disembodied hand to the pile where you want to place the card, and click the Select button again to make the play. Click the face-down card (upper left) for three new cards to choose from.

Reading the iPod Battery Meter

The green battery icon on the iPod's screen shows the approximate amount of gas left in the tank. As you use the iPod, the green level begins to creep down. When the battery turns red, it's time to get the iPod to your computer or an electrical outlet (if you have an optional AC adapter) for a fill-up.

When the iPod's connected to the computer, the battery icon displays a charging animation, complete with tiny lightning bolt. If the iPod turns off while charging, the battery icon appears in the center of the screen below the word "Charging." When the iPod's juiced up, this changes to the word "Charged."

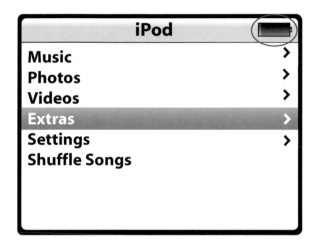

Shuffle owners: your battery indicator's the tiny light next to the Off switch. Green means fully charged, amber means you're getting low, and red means time to fill up.

 Tip The iPod uses a rechargeable lithium ion battery. Battery life depends on which version of the iPod you have and how you use it. You get more battery life listening to music than watching videos or slideshows because that bright color screen is power-mad.

Charging Your iPod Without the Computer

The USB 2.0 cable (or USB Dock, if you have a Shuffle) that comes with your iPod has two jobs:

- To connect your iPod to iTunes.

- To draw power from the computer to charge up the iPod's battery.

There may be times, however, when your iPod's battery is in the red and you're nowhere near your computer. Then it's time to turn to other options, including:

- **Using an Apple iPod USB Power Adapter.** This white box has a jack to plug in your iPod's USB cable (and connected iPod) into the backend. The adapter has a set of silver power prongs that flip up and plug into a regular electrical outlet. You can find the AC adapter for around $29 in iPod-friendly stores or online at *http://store.apple.com*.

- **Getting a car charger that connects to the standard 12-volt power outlet on most car dashboards.** Several companies make auto chargers for the iPod for around $20, and you can find the hardware at stores that sell iPod gear, Apple Stores (including *http://store.apple.com*) and specialty Web shops like Everything iPod (*http://everythingipod.com*).

Locking Up Your Pod

When you turn your iPod's Screen Lock feature on, the screen displays a safe's door icon that stubbornly refuses to go away until you enter your combination. To activate this protective layer:

❶ Choose Extras→Screen Lock.

❷ On the next screen, you have two choices: Set Combination or Turn Screen Lock On. The first time, select Set Combination to create your secret code.

❸ On the next screen, you see the combination dial with four numbers. Using the click wheel, navigate to each box. By spinning the wheel, pick a number from 0 to 9. Press the center button to enter a number and continue until you fill all four boxes.

❹ Now, when you want to lock your 'Pod, choose Extras→Screen Lock→ Turn Screen Lock On→Lock.

The iPod displays the Lock screen—even when it's asleep or connected to a computer—until you enter the right combination with the click wheel. If you enter the wrong digits, the number boxes flash an angry red.

 Note This lock's not foolproof: You (or someone else) can always get into the iPod by connecting it to iTunes.

In Tune with iTunes

If you read Chapter 1 for a speedy way to get your iPod set up and ready to play, you've already dipped a toe in the iTunes waters. But as you may have guessed, beneath its pretty surface, iTunes is a deep well of media-management wonders.

Even without buying music from the online iTunes Store, you can use the program to import music from your CD collection, and add personal ratings, lyrics, and artwork to your song files. Once you check everything into your iTunes library, the program makes it easy to browse and search through all your treasures.

Yes, iTunes is a powerful program. So powerful, in fact, that this chapter is mainly going to focus on introducing you to iTunes most basic and useful tools—everything from flipping through album covers to backing up. Chapter 4 tells you how to make playlists of songs you've added to iTunes, Chapter 5 is all about blowing your bucks in the iTunes Store, and Chapter 6 spotlights the video side of iTunes.

But enough of the introductory blah-blah. Turn the page if you want to get to know iTunes better.

The iTunes Window: An Introduction

iTunes is your iPod's best friend. You can do just about everything with your digital music here, from converting songs on a CD into iPod-ready music files, buying music, listening to Internet radio stations, watching video—and more.

Here's a quick tour of the main iTunes window and what all the buttons, controls, and sliders do.

The Source panel on the left side of iTunes displays all the audio and video you can tap into at the moment. Click a name in the Source column to make the main song-list area change accordingly, like this:

❶ Click any icon in the Library group to see what's in your different media libraries. As you add movies, music, and other stuff to iTunes, click the appropriate icon to find the type of thing—a song, a TV show—you're looking for.

❷ In the Store area, click the icons to shop for new stuff in the iTunes Store or see the list of things you've already purchased.

❸ If a music CD's in your computer's drive it shows up in the Devices area, as will a connected iPod.

❹ In the Shared area, browse the music libraries of other iTunes fans on your network and play their music on your own computer.

❺ The Playlists section is where iTunes keeps all your custom song lists. The Party Shuffle feature, which lets you play DJ, lives here too.

❻ When you click an area of the Source list, iTunes' main window displays all the things in that category—Music, in this case.

The outer edges of the iTunes window are full of buttons and controls. Here's what they do.

❼ Play and pause your current song or video—or jump to the next or previous track. Use the volume slider to adjust the sound level.

❽ The center of the upper pane shows you what song's playing. To the right of that you have handy buttons to change views within the window and a search box for finding songs fast.

❾ At the bottom-left corner are shortcut buttons for (from left to right) making a new playlist, shuffling or repeating your playlists, and displaying album artwork or videos.

❿ The lower-right corner of iTunes lets you show the iTunes Browser or eject a CD or iPod from the computer.

Changing the Look of the iTunes Window

Don't be misled by the brushed-aluminum look of iTunes: You can push and pull various window parts like salt-water taffy.

- Adjust the height of the iTunes Browser—the three-pane wide quick-browse area that opens when you click the eyeball icon in the lower-right corner—by dragging the tiny dot at the bottom of the Browser up or down.

- The main song list is separated into columns, which you can sort or rearrange. Click a column title (like Name or Artist) to sort the list alpha-betically. Click anywhere in the column title to reverse the sorting order. Change the order of the columns by dragging them.

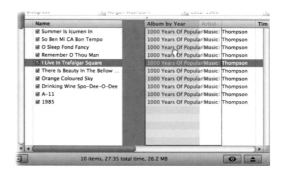

- To adjust a column's width, drag the right-hand vertical divider line. (You may need to grab the line in the column title bar.)

- To resize all columns so their contents fit precisely, right-click (Control-click) any title and choose Auto Size All Columns. Double-clicking a vertical column line does the same for individual columns.

- To add (or delete) columns, right-click (Control-click) any column title. From the pop-up list of column categories (Bit Rate, Date Added, and so on), choose the column name you want to add or remove. Checkmarks indicate currently visible columns.

Changing the Size of the iTunes Window

Lovely as iTunes is, it takes up a heck of a lot of screen real estate. When you're working on other things, you can shrink it down. In fact, iTunes can run in three size modes: small, medium, or large:

❶ *Large.* What you get the first time you open iTunes.

❷ *Medium.* Switch back and forth between large and medium by pressing Ctrl+M or choosing Advanced→Switch to Mini Player. If you use iTunes on a Mac, click the green zoom button at the top-left corner (or choose Window→Zoom).

❸ *Small.* To really scrunch things down, start with the medium-size window. Then drag the resize handle (the diagonal lines in the lower-right corner) leftward. To expand it, just reverse the process.

Tired of losing your mini-iTunes window among the vast stack of open windows on your screen? You can make it so that the iTunes mini-player is *always* visible on top of other open documents, windows, and other screen detritus. Just open iTunes Preferences (Ctrl+comma/⌘-comma), click the Advanced tab, and turn on the checkbox next to "Keep Mini Player on top of all other windows." Now you won't have to click frantically trying to find iTunes if you get caught listening to your bubblegum-pop playlist when you thought nobody was around.

The iTunes Visualizer

Visuals is the iTunes term for an onscreen laser-light show that pulses, beats, and dances in perfect sync to the music you're listening to. The effect is hypnotic and wild. (For real party fun, invite some people who grew up in the 1960s to your house to watch.)

❶ To summon this psychedelic display, choose View→Turn Visualizer On. The show begins immediately.

> **Tip** The keyboard shortcut for turning the Visualizer off and on is Ctrl+T (⌘-T).

❷ You can change the size of your visuals by going to the Preferences box (Ctrl+comma/⌘-comma), clicking the Advanced and then the General tab, and then selecting Small, Medium, or Large from the Visualizer Size pull-down menu. You can also run your visuals full-size, screensaver-style by turning on the checkbox below that menu.

True, you won't get a lot of work done, but when it comes to stress relief, visuals are a lot cheaper than a hot tub.

Picking the Songs You Want to Rip

In Chapter 1 you learned how iTunes simplifies converting (also called *rip-ping*) songs from your compact discs into small iPod-ready digital files: You basically just pop a CD into your computer's disc drive and iTunes walks you through the process. If you're connected to the Internet, iTunes downloads song titles and other album info. A few minutes later, you've got copies of those tunes in iTunes.

If you want time to think about *which* songs you want from each CD, tweak iTunes import preferences so that, initially, you just download the song titles. Simply summon the Preferences box (Ctrl+comma/⌘-comma), click the Advanced tab, followed by the Importing tab, and then change the menu next to "On CD insert:" to "Show CD."

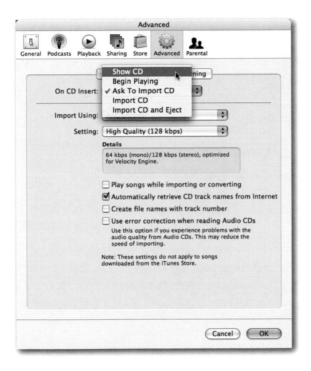

Tip If you know you want all the songs on that stack of CDs next to your computer, just change the iTunes CD import preferences to "Import CD and Eject" to save yourself some clicking.

So now, if you don't want the entire album—who wants anything from Don McLean's *American Pie* besides the title track?—you can exclude the songs you *don't* want by removing the checkmarks next to their names. Once you've picked your songs, in the bottom-right corner of the screen, click the Import CD button.

You can Ctrl+click (⌘-click) any box to deselect all checkboxes at once. To do the reverse, Ctrl+click (⌘-click) a box next to an unchecked song to turn them all on again. This is a great technique when you want only one or two songs in the list; turn *all* checkboxes off, and then turn those *two* back on again.

As the import process starts, iTunes moves down the list of checked songs, ripping each one to a file in your My Documents→My Music→iTunes→iTunes Music folder (Home→Music→iTunes→iTunes Music). An orange squiggle next to a song name means the track is currently converting. Feel free to switch to other programs, answer email, surf the Web, and do other work while the ripping is under way.

Once the importing's done, each imported song bears a green checkmark, and iTunes signals its success with a little melodious flourish. Now you have some brand-new files in your iTunes music library.

Changing Import Settings for Better Audio Quality

The iPod can play several different digital audio formats: AAC, MP3, WAV, AIFF, and a newer format called Apple Lossless. This may not mean anything to you unless you *don't* like the way your music sounds on the iPod or a pair of external speakers.

If you find the audio quality lacking, change the way iTunes encodes, or *rips*, those tracks during the CD conversion process. iTunes gives you two main options in its import settings box (Edit [iTunes]→Preferences→Advanced→ Importing):

- **Format (pull-down menu: "Import Using").** Some formats tightly compress audio data to save space. The tradeoff: lost sound quality. Highly compressed formats include AAC (iTunes' default setting) and MP3. Formats that use little or no compression include WAV and AIFF, which sound better, but take up more space. Apple Lossless splits the difference: Better sound quality than AAC and MP3, but not as hefty as WAV or AIFF.

- **Bit rate ("Setting").** The higher the number of bits listed, the greater the amount of data contained in the file, and the better the sound quality in your ears.

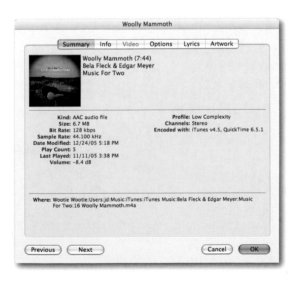

To see a song's format, click its title in iTunes, press Ctrl+I (⌘-I), and then click the Summary tab in the Get Info box.

Three Ways to Browse Your Collection

Instead of just presenting you with boring lists of songs and albums, iTunes gives you three options for browsing your media collection—some of them more visual than others. Click the View button at the top of iTunes to switch between the different views.

- **List** presents the traditional way of seeing your song titles. Click the eyeball-shaped Browser button at the bottom of the iTunes window to see a new window pane that groups your music by Artist, Album, and even Genre.

- **Grouped with Artwork** gets you a list of music that also includes an album cover, (if you have one for that album) next to the song titles. This view works best when you sort by Album, because if you sort by Song title, you get a long list of album covers, each with one lonely song huddled up against it.

- **Cover Flow.** If you like album art, this view's for you. In the top part of iTunes, your collection appears as a stream of album covers. To browse your music, press the left and right arrow keys on the keyboard or drag the scroll bar underneath the albums to see them whiz by.

Finding Your Songs in iTunes

You can call up a list of all the songs with a specific word in their title, album name, or artist attribution, just by clicking the Music icon under Library and typing a few letters into the Search box in iTunes' upper-right corner. With each letter you type, iTunes shortens the list of songs that are visible, displaying only tracks that match what you've typed.

For example, typing *train* brings up a list of everything in your music collection that has the word "train" somewhere in the song's information—maybe the song's title ("Love Train"), the band name (Wire Train), or the Steve Earle album (*Train A Comin'*). Click the other Library icons like Movies or Audiobooks to search those collections for titles that match your search terms.

Another way to search for specific titles is to use the iTunes Browser mentioned earlier in this chapter. Click the eyeball-shaped icon down in the bottom corner of iTunes to reveal your collection grouped by Artist and Album. Click the eyeball again to close the Browser.

 Tip You can add a Genre pane to your iTunes browser by going to the Preferences box (Ctrl+comma/⌘-comma) and turning on the checkbox next to "Show genre when browsing."

Shuffling Your Music...and Smart Shuffle

With its sometimes uncanny ability to randomly pluck and play songs that just seem perfect together, the Shuffle feature has won over a huge number of fans, especially those who don't want to think about what to listen to as they noodle around the Internet. To start shuffling just click the twisty arrows icon down on the bottom-left corner of the iTunes window.

But, sometimes, the random shuffling can be a bit jarring, especially if you have a wide range of music crammed onto your hard drive and the buzz saw screech of a classic punk track doesn't provide the sonic segue you were looking for after that delicate Vivaldi concerto.

Fortunately, iTunes lets you control some of the unpredictability of your random song shuffling with the Smart Shuffle setting in the program's Preferences box (Ctrl+comma/⌘-comma). Just click the Playback tab and then, within the Smart Shuffle area, tell iTunes to shuffle songs, whole albums, or groupings (often used by classical music fans to round up all the parts of a particular symphony on a disc full of multiple symphonies).

If you click the button for Albums or Groupings when adjusting your preferences in the Smart Shuffle area, iTunes will play all the songs on that album or within that grouping in the order they appear on the album without mixing up the tracks within the album or grouping. Once iTunes has played all the songs on the album or in the group, it randomly starts playing another whole album or song grouping.

You can also tinker with fate and use the Smart Shuffle slider to increase or decrease the probability that iTunes will play tracks from the same album or artist back to back, instead of jumping all around your library. Just nudge the slider toward "more likely" or "less likely" to hear consecutive tracks from the same singer. This can be helpful if you secretly hope to hear a few Gwen Stefani tracks in a row before iTunes moves on to something else.

You're the Critic: Rating Your Songs

Although there's no way to give a song two thumbs up within iTunes, you can assign each song in your collection a star rating (one to five). Then you can use your personal ratings to easily produce nothing but playlists of hits.

❶ To add a rating to a song, first make sure the My Rating column is turned on in the iTunes Options box (Ctrl+J [⌘-J]).

❷ In the My Rating column (in the iTunes main window), drag the mouse across the column to create one to five stars.

❸ Once you've assigned ratings, you can sort your list by star rating (click the My Rating column title), create a Smart Playlist of only your personal favorites (File→New Smart Playlist; choose My Rating from the first drop-down menu), and so on.

You can even rate songs on the iPod and your ratings will transfer back to iTunes when you sync up. To rate a song on the iPod, start playing it and tap the Select button a few times until you see shadowy dots on screen. Use the scroll wheel to transform the dots into the number of stars you feel the song deserves.

Listening to Internet Radio

Not satisfied with being a mere virtual jukebox, iTunes also serves as an international radio without the shortwave static. You can find everything from mystical Celtic melodies to Zambian hip hop.

Computers with high-speed Internet connections have a smoother streaming experience, but the vast and eclectic mix of music is well worth checking out—even with a dial-up modem. Just click the Radio icon in the Source list to see a list of stations.

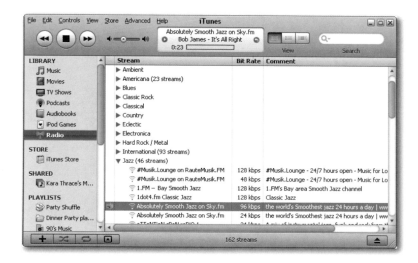

If you find your radio streams are constantly stuttering and stopping, summon the Preferences box (Ctrl+comma/⌘-comma). On the Advanced tab, click the General icon or tab. Then, from the Streaming Buffer Size pop-up menu, choose Large. Click OK.

Having the buffer set to Large may increase the waiting time before the music starts playing, but it allows iTunes to hoard more music at once to help make up for interruptions caused by network traffic.

Once you've listened to all the stations listed in iTunes, hit the Internet. You can find more radio stations at sites like *www.shoutcast.com* and you can play them through iTunes when you click the link to listen. (You may need to double-click an automatically downloaded *.pls* file—that's the iTunes playlist extension—in order to start the broadcast).

Sharing Your Music

Now that you've built a fabulous music collection, you may feel like sharing it. You can, under a couple of conditions:

- The people you want to share with are on the same part of your computer network.

- You set up your iTunes preferences to share music.

To "publish" your tunes to the network, call up the Preferences box (Ctrl+comma/⌘-comma) and then click the Sharing tab. Turn on "Share my library on my local network." You can choose to share your entire collection or just selected playlists. (You can also tell your own computer to look for other people's Shared music here, too).

Whatever you type in the "Shared name" box will show up in your friend's iTunes Source list. You can also require a password to your own music library—a handy feature if you feel folks mooch off of you quite enough.

It's easy to listen to somebody else's music collection; once it's been shared, their iTunes libraries generally appear right in your Source list. Double-click the desired song to fire it up and play through your computer's speakers. (If your pal has put a password on the shared collection, you'll have to type that in before you can listen.)

Changing a Song's File Format

Sometimes you've got a song already in iTunes whose format you want to change—maybe you need to convert an AIFF format file before loading it onto your iPod Shuffle. First, head over to Edit→Preferences (iTunes→Preferences), click the Advanced tab and then the Importing tab. From the Import Using pop-up menu, pick the format you want to convert *to* and then click OK.

Now, in your iTunes library, select the song you want to convert and then choose Advanced→Convert Selection to AAC (or MP3, AIFF, or whatever format you just picked).

If you have a whole folder or disk full of potential converts, hold down the Shift (Option) key as you choose Advanced→Convert to AAC (or your chosen encoding format). A window pops up, which you can use to navigate to the folder or disk holding the files you want to convert. The only files that don't get converted are protected ones: Audible.com tracks and AAC songs purchased from the iTunes Store.

The song or songs in the original format, as well as the freshly converted tracks, are now in your library.

Evening Out Your Song Volumes

No longer must you strain to hear delicate Chopin piano compositions on one track, only to suffer from melted eardrums when Slayer kicks in on the next track. The Sound Check feature attempts to even out disparate volumes, making softer songs louder and gently lowering the real screamers in your library. Audiophiles may nitpick about the Sound Check function, but it can be quite useful, especially for times—like bicycling uphill—when constantly grabbing at the iPod's volume controls is inconvenient.

The first step to using Sound Check is to turn it on. In iTunes, open the Preferences box (Ctrl+comma/⌘-comma). Click the Playback icon or tab and turn on the box for Sound Check.

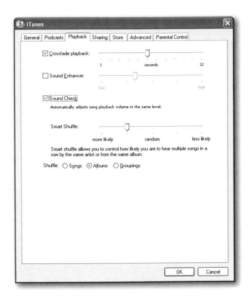

You also need to turn on Sound Check on the iPod itself: From the iPod's main screen, choose Settings→Sound Check and click the Select button. The next time you connect the iPod to the computer, iTunes will make the necessary audio adjustments to protect your ears.

 Tip In that same Playback Preferences box, you can fiddle with the Sound Enhancer slider, which is supposed to add "depth" to your music (try it to see if it does) and overlap the beginnings and endings of your songs, DJ-style with the Crossfade Playback slider.

Improving Your Tunes with the Graphic Equalizer

If you'd like to improve the way your songs sound, use iTunes' graphic equalizer (EQ) to adjust various frequencies in certain types of music—say, higher bass frequencies to emphasize the booming rhythm for dance tracks.

To get the Equalizer front and center, choose View Show→Equalizer and unleash some of your new EQ powers.

❶ Drag the sliders (bass on the left, treble on the right) to accommodate the strengths and weaknesses of your speakers or headphones (and listening tastes). You can drag the Preamp slider up or down to help compensate for songs that sound too loud or soft. To design your own custom preset pattern with the Preamp and the other 10 sliders, click the pop-up menu and select Make Preset.

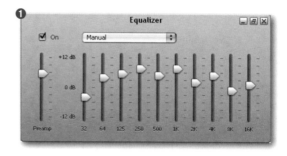

 Equalization is the art of adjusting the frequency response of an audio signal. An equalizer emphasizes or boosts some of its frequencies while lowering others. In the range of audible sound, *bass* frequency is the low rumbly noise; *treble* is at the opposite end with the high, even shrill sound; and *midrange* is, of course, in the middle, and it's the most audible to human ears.

❷ Use the pop-up menu to choose one of the canned presets designed for Classical, Dance, Jazz, and so on.

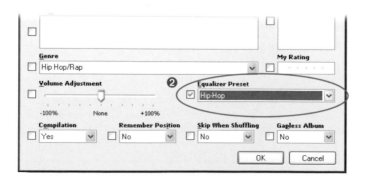

You can apply the same equalizer setting to an entire album or you can select different settings for individual songs.

❸ To apply settings to a whole album, select the album's name in the iTunes browser window (click the eyeball at lower-right to summon the browser) and then press Ctrl+I (⌘-I). In the box that pops up, choose your preferred setting from the Equalizer Preset pull-down menu.

❹ You can apply these equalizer presets to specific songs as well. Instead of selecting the album name, click the song name in the iTunes window, and then press Ctrl+I (⌘+I). Click the Options tab and choose a setting from the Equalizer Preset menu.

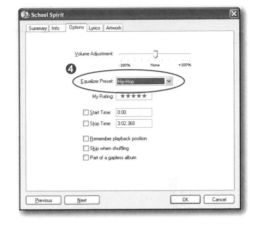

❺ You can also make an Equalizer pop-up tab appear as one of the iTunes columns. Choose Edit→View Options and turn on the Equalizer checkbox. A new column appears right in iTunes from which you can change your EQ settings.

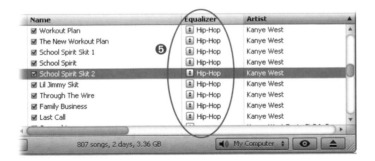

Tip The iPod itself has more than 20 equalizer presets you can use on the go. To set your iPod's Equalizer to a preset designed for a specific type of music or situation, choose iPod→Settings→EQ. Scroll down the list of presets until you find one that matches your music style, and then press the Select button. The name of the preset is now listed next to EQ on the Settings menu.

Finding (and getting rid of) Duplicate Songs

Accidentally pulled more than one copy of *Yesterday* into iTunes and find yourself lamenting the wasted megabytes of precious hard drive space? Put iTunes on Double Duty—you can have the program seek out and round up duplicate songs—just click the Library icon or a playlist icon in the iTunes Source list, and choose View→Show Duplicates.

After iTunes locates all the dupes, it shows them in its main window with a notice at the bottom that reads, "Displaying Duplicates." Here, you can look through and delete extra copies you don't need. But before you start whacking away, make sure these are true duplicates—and not two versions of the same tune by different people, two separate performances (like a live and a studio version of the same ditty), or a version of the same song from its original album and one from a soundtrack compilation.

Once you've cleaned up your library, at the bottom of the iTunes window, click Show All to clear out the list of duplicates and show your full collection in all its glory.

Changing a Song's Start and Stop Times

Got a song with a bunch of onstage chitchat before the music starts? Fortunately, you don't have to sit there and listen. You can change the start and stop times of a song so you hear only the juicy middle part.

As you play the song you want to adjust, observe the iTunes status display window; watch for the point in the timeline where you get bored. Then:

❶ Click the track you want to adjust.

❷ Choose File→Get Info to call up the information box for the song.

❸ Click the Options tab and take a look at the Stop Time box, which shows the full duration of the song.

❹ Change the number to the length of time you want the song to run, as you noted earlier.

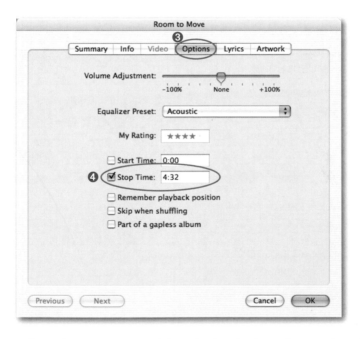

(You can perform the exact same trick at the beginning of a song by adjusting the time value in the Start Time box.) The shortened version plays in iTunes and on the iPod, but the additional recorded material isn't really lost. If you ever change your mind, go back to the song's Options box, turn off the Stop Time box, and return the song to its full length.

Editing Song Information

You have a couple of different ways to change song titles in iTunes—for example, to fix a typo or other incorrect information.

In the song list, click the text you want to change, wait a moment, and then click again. The title now appears highlighted and you can edit the text—just like when you change a file name on the desktop.

Another way to change the song's title, artist name, or other information is to click the song in the iTunes window and press Ctrl+I (⌘-I) to bring up the Get Info box. (Choose File→Get Info if you forget the keyboard shortcut.) Click the Info tab and type in the new track information.

 Tip Once you've got a song's Get Info box on screen, use the Previous and Next buttons to navigate to the other tracks grouped with it in the iTunes song list window. This way, if you want to rapidly edit all the track information on the same playlist, on the same album, and so on, you don't have to keep closing and opening each song's Get Info box.

Editing Album Information

You don't have to adjust your track information on a song-by-song basis. You can edit all the tracks on an album at once by clicking the Album name in the iTunes browser and pressing Ctrl+I (⌘-I) to bring up the Get Info box.

Ever careful, iTunes flashes an alert box asking if you really want to change the info for a bunch of things all at once. Click Yes.

You can make all sorts of changes to an album in the Multiple Item Information box that pops up. Here are just a few examples:

❶ Fix a typo or mistake in the Album or Artist name boxes.

❷ Manually add an album cover or photo of your choice to the whole album by dragging it into the Artwork box.

❸ Change the Equalizer preset for all the songs.

❹ Have iTunes skip the album when you're shuffling music—which can keep winter holiday music out of your summer barbecue album rotation.

❺ Tell iTunes to play back the album without those two-second gaps between tracks by choose the Gapless Album option. (Great for opera and *Abbey Road*!)

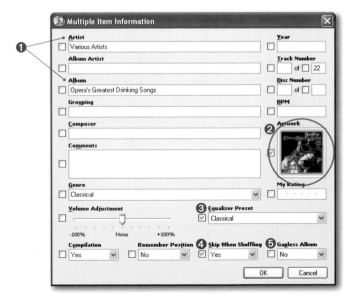

Adding Artwork Automatically

Songs you download from the iTunes Store often include artwork—usually a picture of the album cover. iTunes displays the picture in the lower-left corner of its main window (you may need to click the Show Artwork icon at lower left). Covers also appear in both the Grouped with Artwork and the Cover Flow views. But even if you ripped most of your music from your own CDs, you're not stuck with artless tracks. In iTunes 7 and later, you can have the program go out over the Internet and try to find as many album covers for your music as it can.

You need to have a (free) iTunes Store account to make this work, so if you haven't signed up yet, skip over to Chapter 5 to learn how. To make iTunes go fetch, choose Advanced→Get Album Artwork.

Then go fetch yourself a sandwich while iTunes gets to work. If you have a huge library, this may take a little while. When iTunes gets done, though, you should have a healthy dose of album art whizzing by in Cover Flow view or peeping out of the artwork pane in the lower-left corner of iTunes.

 Note Apple gives you a warning box for this procedure, since iTunes has to root around in your library, see what you have, and then report it all to Apple to request the art. An alert box pops up the first time you ask for art, just so you know it's not a completely private procedure. (Don't worry, though, Apple isn't laughing at your Bay City Rollers collection.)

Adding Artwork Manually

Despite its best intentions, sometimes iTunes can't find an album cover (or retrieves the wrong one). If that happens, take matters into your own hands by manually adding your own album artwork—or even the photo of your choice instead. If Pachelbel's *Canon in D* makes you think of puppies, you can have baby dachshund photos appear in iTunes every time you play that song.

❶ To add your own art to a song, pick a photo or image—JPEG files are the most common.

❷ If you found the right album cover on Amazon.com or another Web site, save a copy of the image by dragging it off the Web page to your desktop or right-clicking and choose the "Save Image" option in your Web browser.

❸ With your image near the iTunes window, select the song and click the Show Artwork button in the bottom-left corner of the iTunes window.

❹ Drag the image file into the Artwork pane in iTunes to add it to the song file.

Tip You can also click a song title, type Ctrl+I (⌘-I) to bring up the Get Info box, and then click the Artwork tab. Then just click the Add button to call up a navigation box that lets you choose an image from your hard drive.

Finding and Adding Lyrics to Your Song Files

You can store a song's lyrics inside the song file just as you do with album art. To add lyrics to a song, select it in iTunes and press Ctrl+I (⌘-I) to call up the song's Info box. Then click the Lyrics tab.

Here, you can either meticulously type in the verses to the song or look them up on one of the hundreds of Web sites around the Net that are devoted to cataloging song lyrics. Once you find your words, getting them into the iTunes Lyrics is merely a cut 'n' paste job away. If you want to add lyrics to all the songs on an album or have several to do on the same playlist, click the Next button at the bottom of the window to advance to the next song to save yourself repeated keystrokes invoking the Get Info command.

> **Tip** Some types of iTunes files don't support the lyrics function. AAC and MP3 are perfectly happy with lyrics, but QuickTime and WAV files can't handle words, so you need to convert that WAV of "Jumping Jack Flash" if you want to have a gas, gas, gas with lyrics.

Viewing Artwork and Lyrics on the iPod

Now that you've spent all this time grooming your song files and adding art and words, wouldn't it be great if you could take the fruits of your labor with you? The good news is you can—all the info in the iTunes song files transfers over when you copy the tracks to your iPod. Except, of course, if you have an iPod Shuffle, which lacks the whole screen thing needed to view images and text.

When you're out strolling with the iPod, press the center button while a song is playing to cycle through all the information about the song. After three or four taps, artwork and then lyrics appear on the iPod's screen, making it a handheld karaoke machine you can dance down the street with.

What iTunes Can Tell You About Your iPod

iTunes not only lets you decide which songs and videos end up on your iPod, it also helps keep your iPod's own internal software up to date, see how much space you have left on your player, and change your music, video, and podcast synchronization options.

When you plug your iPod into the computer with its USB cable and it shows up in the iTunes Source list (in the Devices area), click the iPod icon to see all these options. Each tab at the top of the screen lets you control a different element on your iPod, like Music, Photos, or Games.

Here on the Summary screen, iTunes tells you:

❶ The size of your iPod, its serial number, and if it's formatted for Windows or Macintosh.

❷ If your iPod has the latest software (or if it's having problems, the chance to reinstall its software).

❸ If your iPod is set to automatically synchronize with the iTunes library or have its contents updated manually by you. (Automatic means everything in iTunes ends up on your iPod—space permitting, of course; manual means you get to pick and choose.)

Using iTunes to See What's on Your iPod

iTunes gives you two ways to quickly see what digital goodies are loaded on your iPod. That info's important if you sync your iPod manually and can't remember if you copied a particular album or video over to the iPod. It's also helpful if you want to load a bunch of new movies, or other space-hogging files, and aren't sure how much room you've got left on your iPod.

- To see what's on your iPod, click the flippy triangle next to the iPod's icon in the iTunes Source list. Then click any category—Music, Movies, and so on—to have iTunes display all the stuff under the selected category.

- Click the iPod's icon and then click the Summary tab in the main window to see a color graphic displaying how much of your iPod is filled with audio, video, photos, and so on. If you want more information than say, "12.5 gigabytes," click the colored bar itself to see the statistics change to the number of items in each category (like 440 photos or 3396 songs), or how many hours (even *days*) worth of each type of media your iPod is holding for you.

Adjusting Your iPod's Preferences with iTunes

Once your iPod's connected and showing up in iTunes, you can modify all the settings that control what goes on and off your media player. See all those tabs in a row towards the top of iTunes? Click each one to get to those specific preferences. Here's what to find in each area (if you don't see every tab, you've got a Nano or a Shuffle):

❶ **Summary.** Key iPod hardware info here: Drive capacity, serial number, and software version (and a button to update the same when Apple releases a new version). The Options area lets you choose syncing options and whether to turn your iPod into a portable data drive for carrying around big files.

❷ **Music.** Click this tab to synchronize all songs and playlists—or just the ones you tinker with the most.

❸ **Movies.** Full-length movies can take up a gigabyte or more of precious 'Pod space, so iTunes gives you the option of loading up all, selected, or even just unwatched films.

❹ **TV Shows.** As with Movies, you can selectively choose which TV Shows you want to bring along on your iPod.

❺ **Podcasts.** Your pal iTunes can automatically download the podcasts you've *subscribed* to through the iTunes Store (Chapter 5); here you can decide which ones you want to listen to on the go.

❻ **Photos.** The iPod and iPod Nano can both display little copies of your digital photos. Click this tab to select where you want iTunes to look for photos (like in iPhoto or Photoshop Elements) and which specific albums you want.

❼ **Contacts.** It's not just an all-purpose media player! The iPod is happy to carry copies of all addresses and phone numbers in your computer's address book (from Microsoft Outlook, the Mac OS X Address Book, and other programs). Scroll down the screen and there's an option to grab Outlook or iCal calendars, too.

❽ **Games.** You get a few basic built-in iPod games in your Extras menu, but if you've purchased *Pac-Man* or *Bejeweled* from the iTunes Store, you can decide which ones to move to your iPod.

Loading Songs on an iPod from More Than One Computer

iTunes' *Autosync* feature makes keeping your iPod up-to-date a total breeze, but there's a big catch: You can sync your iPod with only one computer. Lots of people have music scattered around multiple machines: a couple of different family Macs, an office PC and a home PC, and so on. If you want to load up your music from each one of these, you have to change the iPod to manual management. That's easy to do. Just connect the iPod, select it in the Source list, and then click the Summary tab in the iTunes window. Then:

- Scroll down to the Options area and turn on the checkbox next to "Manually manage music and videos." Click the Apply button in the bottom corner of iTunes to make the change.

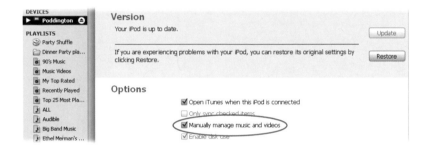

- From now on you'll have to manually eject the iPod from iTunes every time you want to remove it from your computer. (Manual update gives you total control, but as Uncle Ben said in *Spider-Man*, "With great power comes great responsibility.") Eject the iPod by either clicking the Eject button next to its name in the iTunes Source list or clicking the Eject iPod button down in the bottom corner of iTunes.

Tip Your iPod's Summary screen (in iTunes) shows whether the iPod's formatted for Mac or Windows. If you have a new iPod and want to use it with both a Mac and a PC, connect it to the PC first and have iTunes format the iPod for Windows. A Mac can read the Windows format just fine, but Windows won't recognize the Mac format without special software.

Manually Deleting Music and Videos from Your iPod

People who choose to autosync their iPods don't have to worry about dumping stuff off their players. They can choose which playlists and media to automatically copy over to the iPod—or they can just delete unwanted items out of iTunes and resync to wipe the same files off the player.

If you're a Manual Manager, you have to delete unwanted files yourself. (You can, however, have iTunes automatically update your podcast subscriptions for you; see Chapter 5 for more about podcasts.)

❶ To delete files from your iPod, connect it to the computer, and click the iPod icon in the Source list.

❷ Click the flippy triangle next to the iPod icon to get to the media library you want to clean up. (The triangle disappears once you click it.) If you want to delete some songs, for example, click the Music icon.

❸ In the list that appears on the right side of iTunes, select the unwanted songs and press the Delete key on the keyboard. This removes the files from your iPod, but doesn't whack them out of the iTunes library.

Automatically Loading Your iPod Shuffle

You can't stuff your entire music library onto your Shuffle, but you can Autofill it with a Shuffle-sized serving of tunes. Once you plug your player into the computer, a small panel appears at the bottom of iTunes, inviting you to fill your iPod up with the click of the Autofill button.

You can snag songs from your entire library or just a particular playlist; you can also opt to have iTunes select highly rated songs more often.

The Autofill box also has a setting called "Choose items randomly." Turning this checkbox on means iTunes moves over songs in whatever order it feels like, instead of transferring them in the same order they appear in the iTunes Library or a selected playlist.

Once you've Autofilled for the first time and then return for another batch of songs, you can turn on the checkbox next to "Replace all items when Autofilling" to have iTunes wipe the first batch of songs off the Shuffle and substitute new tracks.

Once iTunes has filled up the Shuffle, you'll see the "OK to Disconnect" at the top of iTunes. Click the Eject button next to your Shuffle's icon, and then unplug the player from the computer.

Manually Adding Music to the iPod Shuffle

If you want to decide what goes on your Shuffle, you can opt for manual updating instead of letting iTunes choose. As with any other iPod on manual control, you can drag songs and playlists from your iTunes library and drop them on the Shuffle's icon in the Source list.

When you've clicked the Shuffle's icon, feel free to arrange individual songs into the order you want to hear them—just drag them up or down. The info down at the bottom of the iTunes window tells you how much space you've got left on your Shuffle if you're looking to fill it to the rim.

You can also mix and match your song-loading methods. Start by dragging a few favorite playlists over to the Shuffle, and then click Autofill to finish the job. Just make sure the "Replace all songs when Autofilling" checkbox isn't turned on or iTunes wipes off all those tracks you personally added.

While regular hard drive iPods set to manual update can collect songs from multiple computers—say, your work and home PCs—the stubborn Shuffle is much more monogamous and demands to be associated with only one computer at a time.

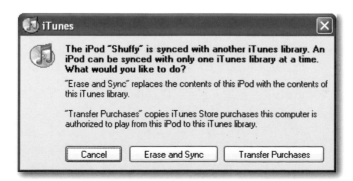

Where iTunes Stores Your Files

Behind its steely silver-framed window, iTunes has a very precise system for keeping your music, movies, and everything else you've added organized. Inside its own iTunes folder on your hard drive (which, unless you've moved it, is in My Documents→My Music→iTunes [Home→Music→iTunes]), the program stores all your files and song information.

Inside this iTunes folder is your iTunes Library file, a database that contains the names of all the songs, playlists, videos, and other content you've added to iTunes. Be very careful not to move or delete this file if you happen to be poking around in the iTunes folder. If iTunes can't find its Library file, it gives a little sigh and just creates a new one—a new one which doesn't have a record of all your songs and other media goodies.

Even if you accidentally delete the Library file, your music is still on the computer—even if iTunes doesn't know it. That's because all the song files are actually stored in the iTunes Music folder, which is also inside the main iTunes folder. You may lose your custom playlist if your Library file goes missing, but you can always add the music files back and recreate your library.

Moving Your iTunes Music Folder

Music libraries grow large and hard drives can seem to shrink as thousands of songs begin to fill up the space. You may, in fact, be thinking of getting a big external hard drive to use for iTunes storage. That's just dandy, but you need to make sure iTunes knows what you intend to do.

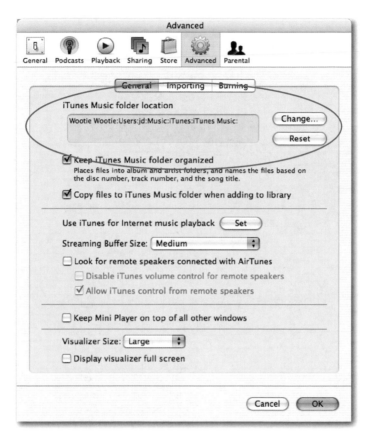

If you rudely drag the iTunes Music folder to a different place without telling iTunes, it thinks the songs are gone. The next time you start the program, you'll find it empty. (While iTunes remains empty but calm, *you* may have heart palpitations as you picture your music collection vanishing in a puff of bytes.)

To move the iTunes Music folder to a new drive, just let the program know where you're putting it. Move the folder to the desired location, then, in the Preferences box (Ctrl+comma/⌘-comma), click the Advanced icon or tab. In the area labeled "iTunes Music folder location," click the Change button, and navigate to the place where you moved the iTunes Music folder. Finally, click OK.

Backing Up Your iTunes Files

If your hard drive dies and takes the whole iTunes folder with it, you lose your music. This can be especially painful if you paid for lots of songs and videos from the iTunes Store, because Apple won't let you re-download new copies. Luckily, iTunes 7 and later gives you a super simple way to back up your iTunes files onto a CD or DVD.

❶ In iTunes, choose File→Back Up to Disc.

❷ In the box that pops up, choose what you want to back up—everything or just items you paid for in the iTunes Store. Later, after you've backed up for the first time, you can turn on the checkbox for backing up only new stuff that you've added since last backing up.

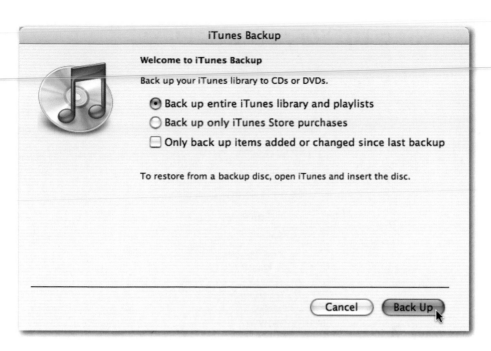

❸ Have a stack of discs ready to feed into your computer's disc drive. Depending on the size of your library, you may need several CDs (which store up to 700 megabytes of data each) or DVDs (which pack in at least 4.7 gigabytes of files per disc). You'll get nagged by iTunes to feed it a new disc when it's filled up the first one.

If you ever need to use your backup, open iTunes, put in a disc and go back to File→Back Up to Disc to start restoring your files.

4

The Power of Playlists

A *playlist* is a group of songs from your iTunes library that you've decided should go together. It can be made up of pretty much any collection of tunes arranged in any order. For example, if you're having a party, you can make a playlist from the current Top 40 and dance music in your iTunes library. If you're in a 1960s Brit Girl Pop mood, you can whip up a playlist that alternates the hits of Dusty Springfield, Lulu, and Petula Clark. Some people may question your taste if you, say, alternate tracks from *La Bohème* with Queen's *A Night at the Opera*, but hey—it's *your* playlist.

Creating playlists has become something of an art form, especially since the iPod arrived in 2001. Several books filled with sample playlists have been published. Academics around the world are writing papers about group dynamics and cultural identity after studying how people make playlists—and which ones they choose to share with others. You can publish your own playlists in the iTunes Store (Chapter 5) so others can witness your mixing prowess. And some nightclubs even invite people to hook up their iPods and share their playlists with the dance-floor audience.

Now that you know what a playlist is and how people use them, it's time to get cracking and make one or 42 of your own.

Making a New Playlist

To create a playlist, press Ctrl+N (⌘-N). You can also choose File→ New Playlist or click the + button below the Source list.

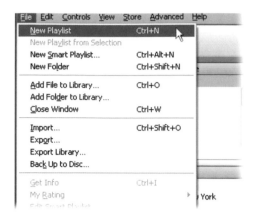

All freshly minted playlists start out with the impersonal name "untitled playlist." Fortunately, its renaming rectangle is open and highlighted—just type a better name: Cardio Workout, Hits of the Highland Lute, or whatever you want to call it. As you add them, your playlists alphabetize themselves in the Playlists area.

Once you've created and named this spanking new playlist, you're ready to add your songs or videos. You can do this in several different ways, so choose the method you like best.

Playlist-Making Method #1

❶ If this is your first playlist, opening the playlist into its own window makes it easy to see what's going on. You get your empty playlist in one window, and your full library in another. To make this happen, just double-click the new playlist's icon in the Source list.

❷ Now drag the song titles you want from the main iTunes window over to the new playlist window. (Make sure you've clicked the Music icon in the Source list to see all your songs.)

Playlist-Making Method #2

❶ Some folks don't like multiple windows. No problem. You can add songs to a playlist by dragging tunes to the playlist's icon right from the main iTunes window.

❷ Tip: If you start accumulating lots of playlists you may need to scroll down to get to your new playlist.

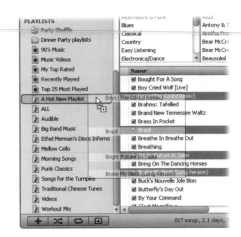

Playlist-Making Method #3

❶ You can also scroll through a big list of songs in your library, selecting tracks as you go by Ctrl+clicking (⌘-clicking) each title.

❷ Then choose File→New Playlist From Selection. All the songs you selected immediately appear in a brand-new playlist.

Don't worry about clogging up your hard drive. When you drag a song title onto a playlist, you don't *copy* the song; you're just giving iTunes instructions about where to find the files. In essence, you're creating an *alias* or *shortcut* of the original. That means you can have the same song on several different playlists.

That nice iTunes even gives you some playlists of its own devising, like "Top 25 Most Played" and "Purchased" (a convenient place to find all your iTunes Store goodies listed in one place).

Changing an Existing Playlist

If you change your mind about a playlist's tune order, just drag the song titles up or down within the playlist window.

You can also drag more songs into a playlist or delete individual titles if you find your playlist needs pruning. (Click the song in the playlist window and then hit Delete or Backspace. When iTunes asks you to confirm your decision, click Yes.) Remember, deleting a song from a playlist doesn't delete it from your music library—it just removes the title from your *playlist*. (You can get rid of a song for good only by pressing Delete or Backspace when the Library *Music* icon's selected.)

You can quickly add a song to an existing playlist right from the main iTunes window, no matter which view you happen to be using: Select the song, Ctrl+click (⌘-click) it, and then, in the pop-up menu, choose "Add to Playlist." Scroll to the playlist you want to use and then let go of the mouse button to add the track to that playlist.

If you want to see how many playlists contain a certain song, select the track, Ctrl+click (⌘-click) it, and choose "Show in Playlist" in the pop-up menu.

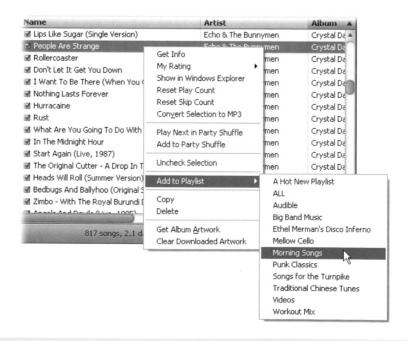

Adding a Playlist to Your iPod

Adding that fabulous new playlist to your iPod doesn't take any heavy lifting on your part. In fact, if you have your iPod set to autosync with iTunes, the only thing you need to do is grab your USB cable and plug in your iPod. Once iTunes recognizes the iPod, it copies any new playlists you've created right over.

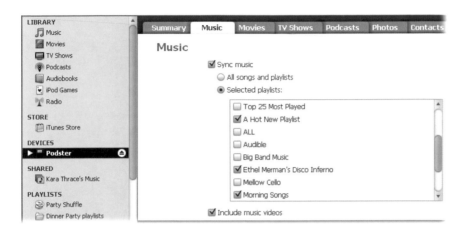

If you share a computer and iTunes library but maintain separate iPods and separate playlists (because you like 1960s show tunes and your spouse prefers speed metal), you can set each iPod to automatically update only *your* chosen playlists. Plug in your iPod and select it in the Source list, and then click the Music tab. In the Sync Music area, click the button for "Selected playlists" and then turn on the checkboxes for the playlists you want *your* iPod to grab.

If you manually manage the syncing process, adding new playlists to your iPod is a total drag, literally—dragging is all you have to do. With your iPod connected and resting comfortably in the Devices area of the iTunes Source list, click the icons for the playlists you want to transfer and drag them onto the iPod's icon. That's it.

Making an On-The-Go Playlist

Sometimes you're out with your iPod, and you get the urge to hear a bunch of songs on different albums one after the other. Good news: You can create a playlist right on your iPod, and have it sync back into iTunes the next time you connect:

❶ Scroll through your iPod until you get to the title of the first song you want to add to the playlist.

❷ Hold down the iPod's center button until the song title flashes quickly three times.

❸ Scroll to the next song and repeat the process.

❹ When you're done adding songs, press the iPod's menu button until you get to the Music menu and go to Playlists→On-The-Go. A list of all the songs you just selected now awaits you.

❺ If you like what you see, scroll down to "Save Playlist" and click the center button. (If you don't like what you see, choose "Clear Playlist" to dump the songs and start over.)

Your freshly inspired playlist now appears in your Playlists menu as New Playlist 1. When you reconnect the iPod to iTunes, you can click the name and change it to something peppier.

Deleting a Playlist

The party's over and you want to delete that iTunes playlist. To delete a playlist, click it in the Source list and press Backspace (Delete). iTunes presents you with a warning box, double-checking that you really want to delete the playlist. (Again, this just zaps the playlist itself, not all the stored songs you had in it. Those are still in your iTunes Music folder.)

If you have your iPod set to autosync, any playlists you delete from iTunes will disappear the next time you plug in your player and it updates its own content to match what you have in iTunes.

If you manually manage your iPod and all its contents, connect the player and spin open the flippy triangle next to its name in the Source list so you can see its libraries and playlists. Click the playlist you want to dump and hit the Backspace (Delete) key on the keyboard.

Party Shuffle: When You Want to Play DJ

The standard iTunes song shuffle feature can be inspiring or embarrassing, depending on which songs the program happens to play. Party Shuffle lets *you* control which songs iTunes selects when it's shuffling at your next wingding. It also shows you what's already been played and what's coming up in the mix, so you'll know what to expect.

❶ **Click the Party Shuffle icon in the Playlists area of the iTunes Source list.** Now you see a new pane at the very bottom of iTunes.

❷ **Use the Source pop-up menu to select a music source for the mix.** You can use either an existing playlist or your whole library.

❸ **Click the Shuffle button at the bottom right of the iTunes window if you don't like the song list that iTunes proposes.** iTunes generates a new list of songs for your consideration.

❹ **Arrange the songs if you feel like it.** You can manually add songs, delete them from the playlist, or rearrange the playing order. To add songs, click the Source list's Music icon and then drag your selected tunes onto the Party Shuffle icon.

❺ **Click the Play button.** And let the music play on.

Smart Playlists: Let iTunes Assemble Your Playlists

Just as you can have iTunes vary your song order, you can also have the program compose playlists all by itself. Once you give it some guidelines, a *Smart Playlist* can go shopping through your music library and come up with its own mix. The Smart Playlist even keeps tabs on the music that comes and goes from your library and adjusts itself on the fly.

You might tell one Smart Playlist to assemble 45 minutes worth of songs that you've rated higher than four stars but rarely listen to, and another to play your most-often-played songs from the 1980s. The Smart Playlists you create are limited only by your imagination.

❶ **To start a Smart Playlist, press Ctrl+Alt+N (Option-⌘-N) or choose File→New Smart Playlist.** A Smart Playlist box opens: It sports a purple gear-shaped icon next to the name in the Source list (a regular playlist has a blue icon with a music note icon in it).

❷ **Give iTunes detailed instructions about what you want to hear.** You can select the artists you want to hear and have iTunes leave off the ones you're not in the mood for, pluck songs that only fall within a certain genre or year, and so on. To add multiple criteria click the plus (+) button.

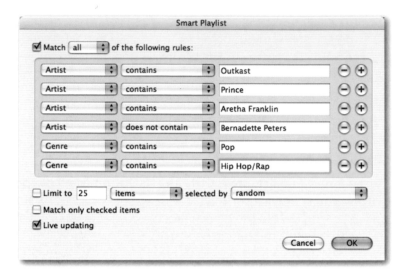

❸ **Turn on the "Live updating" checkbox.** This tells iTunes to keep this playlist updated as your collection, ratings, and play count changes.

❹ **To edit an existing Smart Playlist, right-click (Control-click) the playlist's name.** Then choose Edit Smart Playlist.

A Smart Playlist is a dialogue between you and iTunes: You tell it what you want in as much detail as you want, and the program whips up a playlist according to your instructions.

 Tip When you press Shift (Option), the + button for Add New Playlist at the bottom of the iTunes window turns into a gear icon. Click this gear button to quickly launch the Smart Playlist creation box.

Making Playlist Folders

If you like to have a playlist or five for every occasion, but find your iTunes Source list is getting crowded, iTunes lets you store multiple playlists inside convenient folders.

❶ To add a folder to your Source list, click the Source list's Library icon and choose File→New Folder.

❷ A new "untitled folder" appears, inviting you to change its name to something more original, like Dinner Party Playlists.

❸ Drag any playlists you want to store inside the folder onto its icon.

If the whole family shares one computer, folders can give each person a tidy receptacle to store his or her personal playlists. Folders are also great for storing a bunch of playlists that go great together. That way, when you select the folder and hit play, iTunes plays all the folder's songs consecutively.

But while these Playlists folders are great for bringing order to your iTunes Source list, they don't travel well. When you sync your iPod, a folder's individual playlists all get dumped into one giant playlist bearing the folder's name. This may not matter to some people, but others may find it unbearably messy after all the effort that went into organizing things on the iTunes side of the fence.

Three Kinds of Discs You Can Burn with iTunes

If you want to record a certain playlist on a CD for posterity—or for the Mr. Shower CD player in the bathroom—iTunes gives you the power to burn. In fact, it can burn any of three kinds of discs:

- **Standard audio CDs.** This is the best option: If your computer has a CD burner, it can serve as your own private record label. iTunes can record selected sets of songs, no matter what the original sources, onto a blank CD. When it's all over, you can play the burned CD on any standard CD player, just like the ones from Best Buy—but this time, you hear only the songs you like, in the order you like, with all the annoying ones eliminated.

- **MP3 CDs.** A standard audio CD contains high-quality, enormous song files in the AIFF format. An *MP3* compact disc, however, is a data CD that contains music files in the MP3 format. Because MP3 songs are much smaller than the AIFF files, many more of them fit in the standard 650 or 700 MB of space on a recordable CD. The bottom line? Instead of 74 or 80 minutes of music, a CD full of MP3 files can store *10 to 12 hours* of tunes. The downside? Older CD players may not be able to play these CDs.

- **Backup CDs or DVDs.** If your computer has an optical drive that can play and record both CDs and/or DVDs, you have another option. iTunes can back up your collection by copying it to a CD or DVD, even if you've burned video files on there. (The disc won't play in any kind of player, of course; it's just a glorified backup disk for restoration when something goes wrong with your hard drive.) Chapter 3 tells you how to use data discs to back up your iTunes library.

To see if your disc drive is compatible with iTunes choose Edit→Preferences→ Advanced→Burning (iTunes→Preferences→Advanced→Burning). If your drive name is listed next to "CD Burner," iTunes recognizes it.

 Note Even if you've got a DVD drive, you still see it listed next to the label "CD Burner."

Burning a Playlist to a CD

Pick the type of disc you want to create (see the previous section) in the Preferences dialog box (Ctrl+comma/⌘-comma→Advanced→Burning). Then follow these steps:

❶ **Select the playlist you want to burn.** Check to make sure your songs are in the order you want them; drag any tune up or down to reorder.

❷ **When you're ready to roll, choose File→Burn Playlist to Disc (or click the Burn Disc button).**

❸ **Insert a blank disc into your computer's drive when prompted.** If your computer's got a CD platter that slides out, push it back in. Then sit back as iTunes handles things.

iTunes prepares to record the disc, which may take a few minutes. In addition to prepping the disc for recording, iTunes has to convert the music files (if you're burning an audio CD) to the standard format used by audio CDs.

Once iTunes has taken care of business, it lets you know that it's now burning the disc. Again, depending on the speed of your computer and disc burner, as well as the size of your playlist, the recording process could take several minutes. When the disc is done, iTunes pipes up with a musical flourish. Eject the disc and off you go.

Printing Playlists and Snazzy CD Covers

In earlier versions of iTunes, you had to do a lot of gymnastics just to print a nice-looking song list that would fit into a CD jewel case. With The Modern iTunes of Today, all you need to do is choose File→Print, select a preformatted option, and then click the Print button.

The Print dialog box is *full* of choices.

- You can print out a perfectly sized insert for a CD jewel case, complete with song list on one side and a miniature mosaic of all your album artwork on the other—or just a plain list of songs on a solid color background. (If you choose to make a CD insert, your resulting printout even comes with handy crop marks you can use to guide your X-Acto blade when trimming it down to size.)

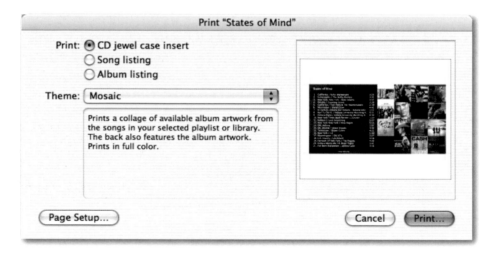

- If you want something simpler, you can opt for a straightforward list of all the songs on the playlist.

- You can also print a list of all the albums that have contributed songs to your playlist, complete with album title, artist name, and the songs' titles and times for each track culled from that particular album.

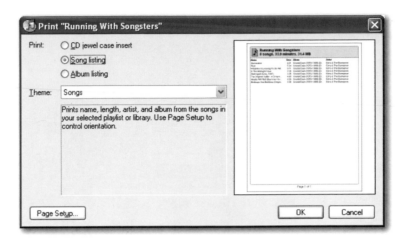

Want to use one of your own personal photos for the cover of your CD case? Just add the artwork of your choice to a track (Chapter 3) and when it comes time to print, select that track on the playlist and then choose File→Print→ Theme: Single Cover to place your photo front and center.

 Want to use that fancy color laser printer at work? If you've got a Mac, you can also save your document as a ready-to-print PDF file with all the text and images in place. Just click Print and, from the dialog box that appears, choose "Save as PDF..." from the left-hand drop-down menu.

5

Shop the iTunes Store

People have been downloading music from the Internet since the 1990s, from sites that were legal and others that were, well, not so much. Music fans loved the convenience, but record companies saw potential profits slipping down millions of modem lines. They fought back by suing file-sharing services and other software companies for aiding and abetting copyright infringement.

The need for a mainstream legal music download site was obvious, but many early efforts resulted in skimpy song catalogs and confusing usage rights. Things changed dramatically in April 2003, when the iTunes Music Store went online. Apple made deals with several major record companies to sell digital versions of popular songs for 99 cents a pop—and you could instantly transfer and play the tunes on your iPod or burn them to a CD. Things have gotten even better since.

Now simply called the iTunes Store, you can find millions of songs, plus full-length movies, TV shows, audio books, podcasts, videogames, music videos, and more on its virtual shelves. It's all custom-tailored for the iPod, and best of all, once you download a title, it's yours to keep. This chapter shows you how to find and use what you're looking for, and get more out of The Store.

Getting to the iTunes Store

Compared to paying for gas, fighting traffic, and finding a parking spot at the mall, getting to the iTunes Store is easy. All you need is an Internet connection and a copy of iTunes running on your computer. Once you're online and looking at iTunes, you can either:

❶ Click the iTunes Store icon in the Source list.

❷ Go to View→Show MiniStore if you want to have a little bit of the Store on screen at all times.

The first method lands you squarely on the Store's main page. The second method opens a new pane at the bottom of iTunes; when you play a song, the MiniStore displays similar items that you can buy with just a few clicks.

Tip Even if you're still paddling around the Net on a dial-up modem, you can shop for audio files in the Store. But you may want to shop first and download everything at the end of your session, since you may have a few hours of download time ahead of you as your purchases squeeze through the telephone line. See "Tips for Dial-Up Music Lovers" later in this chapter.

An Overview of the Store's Layout

The iTunes Store is jam-packed with digital merchandise, all neatly filed under category links along the upper-left side of the main window. Click a link to go to that section of the store: Music, Movies, TV Shows, and so on.

Other links along the left side include Top Movies, Top TV Episodes, and Top Music Videos: all the most popular downloads in the Store at the moment. The right side of the screen displays lists of Top Songs, Top Albums, Top Audiobooks, and Top Podcasts.

The center part of the window highlights the latest specials and releases in the Store. Free song downloads and other offers appear here, too. You'll also see a "Just For You" section, which tries to sell you similar items based on your previous purchases. If you find this too stalker-like, use the link at the bottom of the window to turn it off.

If you're looking for a specific item, the Search box (upper-right corner) lets you hone in on your quest by entering titles, artist names, or other searchable info.

The right side of the window has a helpful box of Quick Links to your Account settings, buying and redeeming iTunes Gift Certificates, technical support, and more.

Navigating the Aisles of the iTunes Store

You navigate the iTunes Music Store aisles just like a Web browser. Most song and artist names are hyperlinked—that is, click their names, or album cover images, to see what tracks are included.

Click the Back button in the Store window to return to the page you were just on, or click the button with the small house on it to jump to the Store's home page.

When you find a performer you're interested in, click the name to see a list of available songs or albums. If you click an album name, all the songs available from it appear, below, in the Details window. Double-click a track title to hear a 30-second snippet. Short previews of items in the Store's audio book and video collection are also available, as are movie trailers.

When browsing the store, you may see a small, gray, circular icon bearing a white arrow in some columns of the Details window. That's the "More Info this way!" button. Click the arrow to jump to a page bearing details about the subject, like a discography page, or the main page of artists for the genre listed.

More info button

Setting Up an iTunes Store Account

Before you can listen to song previews or, of course, buy anything, you need to set up an account with Apple. To do so, click the "Sign In" button on the upper-right corner of the iTunes window.

 Tip America Online members can use their AOL screen names to log into the Store, and then pay for their purchases using their AOL Wallet. See AOL's Help section if you need assistance opening your Wallet.

If you've ever bought or registered an Apple product on the company's Web site, signed up for an AppleCare tech-support plan, have a Mac membership, or used another Apple service, you probably already have the requisite Apple ID. All you have to do is remember the ID (usually your email address) and password.

If you've never had an Apple ID, click Create New Account. The iTunes Store Welcome screen lists the three steps you need to follow:

❶ Agree to the terms for using the Store and buying music.

❷ Create an Apple Account.

❸ Supply a credit card or PayPal account number and billing address.

As your first step to creating an Apple Account, you must read and agree to the long scrolling legal agreement on the first screen. The 23-part statement informs you of your rights and responsibilities as an iTunes Store customer. (It boils down to this: *Thou shalt not download an album, burn it to CD, and then sell bootleg copies of it at your local convenience store.*)

Click the Agree button to move on to step 2. Here, you create a user name, password, and secret question and answer. If you later have to click the "Forgot Password?" button in the Store sign-in box because you've blanked on your password—hey, it could happen—this is the question you'll have to answer to prove that you're you. Apple also requests that you type in your birthday to help verify your identity.

On the third and final screen, provide a valid credit card number with a billing address. Instead of a credit card, you can also use a PayPal account for iTunes purchases.

Click Done. You've got yourself an Apple Account. From now on, you can log into the Music Store by clicking the "Sign In" button in the upper-right corner of the iTunes window.

Changing the Information in Your Apple Account

You can change your billing address, switch the credit card you have on file for Store purchases, or edit other information in your Apple Account without calling Apple. Just start up iTunes, click the Store icon in the Source list, and sign in to your account by clicking the Sign In button in the upper-right corner of the screen.

Once you've signed in, you'll see your account name (email address). Click it. In the box that pops up, re-enter your password and click View Account. If you want to change your password or secret identity-proving question, click the Edit Account Info button. To change your billing address or credit card information, click the Edit Credit Card button. You can also deauthorize all the computers that can play songs purchased with this account (more on when and why you'd want to do *that* later in this chapter).

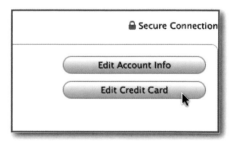

 Note By the way, any changes you make to your Apple Account through iTunes affect other programs or services you may also use with your account, like ordering picture prints with iPhoto (Mac owners only).

Tips for Dial-Up Music Lovers

The fact is, the iTunes Store works best with a high-speed Internet connection. Thanks to Apple's 1-Click option, iTunes can instantly download a selected track as soon as you click the Buy Song button. That's a quick and painless experience for high speeders, but not so much fun for dial-up folks who have to wait for each track to download, bit by painfully slow bit.

If you have a dial-up modem and want a smoother shopping experience, iTunes has a couple of settings that may help. Both are on the Store tab of the iTunes Preferences box (Ctrl+comma/⌘-comma).

❶ **Buy using a Shopping Cart.** Now all songs you buy pile up until the end of your shopping session; then iTunes downloads them all at once when you click the Shopping Cart icon in your iTunes Source list (and then click Buy Now). This way, you can go off and do something productive while the stack of tracks squeezes through the dial-up connection.

❷ **Load complete preview before playing.** This option lets the computer fully download the 30-second song preview before playing it, which helps reduce the fits and starts of streaming music over a slow network connection.

Finding Music by Genre

The main page of the iTunes Store can be a bit overwhelming, especially if you just want to slip in and buy a few Celtic music tracks or browse the latest additions to the Classical section. To quickly find music by genre, click the Music link on the main Store page.

On the left side of the Music page, 20 different musical genres await you, from Alternative to World, with Hip-Hop/Rap, Latin, Jazz, Reggae, and Rock in between. You'll also find a section for Children's Music.

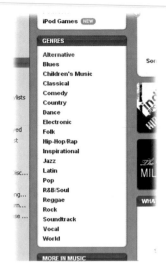

Click one of the genre links and the middle section of the Store window displays all the latest albums in that category, including the newest releases and songs just added to the ever-growing iTunes catalog. The list of top songs, albums, and music videos along the side of the window also changes to reflect the most popular downloads for the genre you've chosen.

Buying a Song or Album

Clicking any album name shows you a list of all the songs available from the record. To purchase any tune, click the Buy Song button in the Price column. You also have the option, in most cases, to buy the whole album with the Buy Album button.

When you download an album, or even just one song, you get music files in the AAC format. A color picture of the album cover is attached to the song file, which appears in iTunes when you're playing the song, or on the color screen of your iPod. Many new albums are also starting to include short music videos and interactive electronic booklets (think liner notes gone digital).

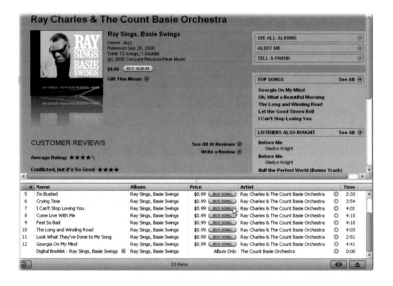

Once you click that Buy Song button, an alert box appears asking if you really want to buy the item you just clicked. Click the glowing Buy button to confirm your purchase decision, or Cancel if you suddenly remember that your credit card is a bit close to the limit this month. Once you click Buy, the download begins and you soon have a new bit of music in your iTunes library.

Buying Movies or Videos

To buy video content, just click the link on the Store's main page for the type you want—a music video, a movie, or a TV show. Apple's full-length movie library is small but growing. You'll see titles like *Pirates of the Caribbean*, *National Treasure*, and a handful of Disney classics like *Dumbo* and *The Little Mermaid*. Compared to little ol' song files, movies can take up a ton of hard drive space—a full gigabyte or more—so be prepared for a download time of 30 minutes or more, depending on your Internet connection.

Dozens of old and new TV classics are also available, including episodes from *Lost, The Daily Show*, and *Law & Order*. You can buy single episodes or entire seasons at once. TV shows are big files, too: one 45-minute episode of *Battlestar Galactica*, for instance, is close to 200 megabytes.

Once you purchase and download the files from the iTunes Store—just click the Buy button next to the title you want—they land in your iTunes Library. If you have a computer with an ultra-zippy USB 2.0 connection, copying videos over to the iPod usually takes a fraction of the time it takes to get them from the Store; transfer times over a USB 1.1 connection can be more tedious.

Buying Audio Books

Some people like the sound of a good book, and iTunes has plenty to offer in its Audiobooks area. You can find verbal versions of the latest bestsellers. Prices depend on the title, but are usually cheaper than buying a hardback copy of the book—which would be four times the size of your iPod anyway. Click any title's name and then the Buy Book button; the rest of the process works just like buying music.

If audio books are your thing, you can find even more of them—all iTunes- and iPod-friendly—at Audible.com (*www.audible.com*), a Web store devoted to selling all kinds of audio books, recorded periodicals like *The New York Times,* and radio shows. To purchase Audible's wares, though, you need to go to the site and create an Audible account. The Audible site has all the details, plus a selection of subscription plans to choose from.

If you use Windows, you'll need to download a small piece of software from Audible called AudibleManager, which slings your Audible files into iTunes. Mac fans don't need to worry about that, as the Audible files land directly in iTunes when you buy them.

Buying iPod Games

If you have a video-playing iPod, you can add to your built-in iPod games (Parachute, Brick, Solitaire, and Music Quiz) with arcade classics like Pac-Man or desktop favorites like Tetris, Zuma, and Bejeweled. Poker fans can pass the time with Texas Hold 'Em, and there's also Mahjong and mini-golf.

Buying and downloading a game is just like buying anything else in the Store. Once you buy a game, it shows up in the iPod Games library in the Source list (click a purchased title to see accompanying directions). After you copy the game to your iPod, you can find it in iPod→Extras→Games. When you start the game, your iPod's scroll wheel and center button are transformed into game controls.

Unlike music or video files, however, you can play iPod games only on the iPod. They don't, alas, work in iTunes.

Downloading and Subscribing to Podcasts

The iTunes Store is host to thousands upon thousands of *podcasts,* those free audio (and video!) programs put out by everyone from big television networks to a guy in his basement with a microphone.

If you want to see what podcasts are available, click the Podcasts link on the Store's main page. You're then whisked to the Podcasts section, where you can browse shows by category, search for podcast names by keyword (use the Search iTunes Store box), or click around until you find something that sounds good.

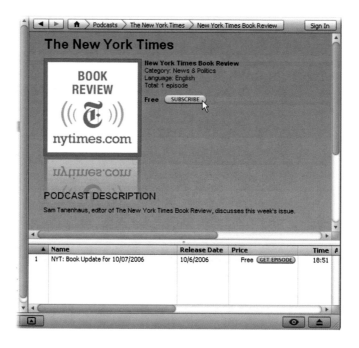

Many podcasters produce regular installments of their shows, releasing new episodes as they're ready. You can have iTunes keep a look out for fresh editions of your favorite podcasts and automatically download them. All you have to do is *subscribe* to the podcast: click the podcast you want, and then click the Subscribe button.

If you want to try out a podcast, click the Get Episode link near its title to download just that one show. Some attention-needy podcast producers don't give you the single-episode download option; in those cases, you'll see a Subscribe Only link near the title.

Usage Rights: What You Can Do with Your Purchases

The stuff you buy at the iTunes Store is yours to keep. You're not charged a monthly fee, and your digitally protected downloads don't go *poof!* after a certain amount of time. Nor do the songs come with such confusing usage rights that you need a lawyer to figure out if you can burn a song to a CD or not. Still, you must follow a few simple rules:

- You can play downloaded songs on up to five different iTunes-equipped Macs or PCs (in any combination) and you can burn them onto CDs (seven times for each playlist).

- You can watch movies, videos, and TV shows on the iPod, on any five computers, or piped over to the TV with an AV cable.

- A single iPod can host purchased items from up to five different accounts, but won't accept any files from a sixth account—a restriction designed to prevent a single iPod from filling up with copyrighted content purchased by, say, members of the entire sophomore class.

You can burn backup CDs and DVDs of your purchases, but you can't burn an iTunes movie or TV show to a disc and watch it on your set-top player.

Publishing Your Own Playlists (iMixes)

An *iMix* is a playlist that you publish on the iTunes Store, so everyone on earth can see your masterwork. You can name it, write your own liner notes explaining your mixing inspiration, and put it out there for everyone to see. (You're not actually copying songs up to the Store; you're just showing off your cool tastes, which Apple hopes will lead others to buy those songs.) Here's how:

❶ Start by signing into your Store account.

❷ Then, in the iTunes Source list, select the playlist you want to publish. (If it contains any songs that Apple doesn't sell, they'll get knocked off the list—which may ruin your carefully constructed mix.)

❸ Choose File→Create an iMix and follow the steps on screen.

❹ Click the Publish button after you fill in all the info about your playlist

Once you click the Publish button, your playlist is released into the wild. Now other people can see your playlist, rate it, be inspired by it, or—and let's face it, here's the main thing—buy the songs for themselves.

Other Cool iTunes Store Features

Apple's loaded the iTunes Store with plenty of unique, ear-inspiring special collections—all designed to separate you from your money. Just click the Music link on the Store's main page and head to the box titled "More in Music":

- **iTunes Collections.** If you're looking for music on a particular theme or from a particular era (like Mardi Gras music or 60's love ditties), an iTunes Collection rounds up a group of tunes to match your interests.

- **iTunes Essentials.** Looking for a quick course in, say, the works of Johnny Cash or Jock Rock Anthems? Usually filled to three levels, starting with well-known works and progressing to more obscure tracks, these playlists are great fun.

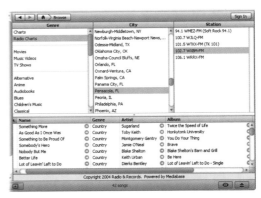

- **Radio Charts.** Here you can literally see what plays in Peoria—or on hundreds of other radio stations around the country.

- **Billboard Charts.** This venerable music magazine has been tracking top singles for years, and has charts dating back to 1946. To find them, click Radio Charts and then, from the Genre pane that appears, select Charts.

- **Celebrity Playlists.** See what the stars are playing on their iPods. Hundreds of actors and musicians share their personally annotated playlists—for better and for worse.

iTunes Gift Certificates: Buying 'Em and Spending 'Em

Gift certificates make perfect presents for people who have everything—especially when purchased by people who are lousy shoppers. These redeemable email coupons are also an excellent way to save face in potentially unpleasant situations. ("Honey, you may think I forgot our anniversary again, but…check your email!")

Buying

To buy one, click Buy & Redeem on the main page of the iTunes Store and then click the Buy button in the Gift Certificates area. After you choose delivery by either email, U.S. Mail, or in person (you can print gift certificates yourself) the process is like buying anything on the Web: you fill in your address, gift amount, personalized message, and so on.

If you already have an Apple ID, you can log in and request to have your credit card billed; if not, sign up for one. Once you complete all the pixel paperwork, your gift certificate will be on its way.

Spending

However they arrive, iTunes Store gift certificates are meant to be spent. Here's how they work:

- If you're lucky enough to be the recipient of an iTunes email gift, redemption is just a click away. Click the Buy & Redeem in the iTunes Store window and then, from the "Buy or Redeem Gift Certificates" box, click Redeem. Copy the Certificate Code from your email and paste it into the box provided. Then start shopping.

Select Delivery Method for Your Gift Certificate

Choose from the options below for how you'd like your iTunes Gift Certificate sent.

Email
Click here to have your Gift Certificate sent via email.

Email

Print
Click here to print your Gift Certificate yourself.

Print

U.S. Mail
Click here to have your Gift Certificate sent via U.S. Mail.

U.S. Mail

Cancel

- If the gift arrived by postal mail, start up iTunes and click iTunes Store in the Source list. On the Store's main page, click the Buy & Redeem link. On the next screen, click Redeem in the Gift Certificates area. Type in the confirmation number printed on the lower edge of the gift certificate and click Redeem.

🔒 Secure Connection

Redeem an iTunes Gift Certificate

Enter your Gift Certificate Confirmation number exactly as it appears on the Gift Certificate you received:

Cancel   Redeem

Buy an iTunes Gift Card ➲

If you already have an iTunes Store account, log in and start shopping. If you've never set your mouse pointer inside the Store before, you'll need to create an Apple Account. You have to provide your name and address, but you don't have to surrender a credit card number. If you choose None, you can use your gift certificate as the sole payment method—and end your shopping experience once you've burned through it.

Other Ways to Send iTunes Gifts

If you want something more personalized than an email message, you have two other options for giving someone an iTunes-themed gift.

The brightly colored prepaid iTunes Music Card is a fun spin on the gift certificate concept. Available in $15, $25, and $50 amounts, givers can find the cards at places like Amazon.com, Target, and Apple's own stores. Recipients can spend it all in one place—the iTunes Store—by clicking the link for iTunes Music Cards on the Store's main page.

In a daring feat of bending a noun into a verb, the iTunes Store also lets you "gift" selections of music and videos to intended recipients, giving them the ability to download your thoughtful picks right from the Store onto their own computers. You can send songs, albums, and playlists to any pal with an email address, as well as audio books, music videos, and TV shows. Just look for the "Gift This…" link on the item's page.

Using iTunes Allowance Accounts

Allowance accounts are a lot like iTunes gift certificates. You, the parent (or other financial authority), decide how many dollars' worth of Store goods you want to give to a family member or friend (from $10 to $200). Unlike gift certificates, however, allowance accounts automatically replenish themselves on the first day of each month—an excellent way to keep music-loving kids out of your wallet while teaching them to budget their money.

Buy Allowance

An iTunes Allowance provides a simple way for family members and friends to buy music without giving them your credit card.

Buy Now

Both you and the recipient need to have Apple IDs. To set up an allowance, from the iTunes Store's main page, click the Buy & Redeem link, click Buy Now (in the Allowance section), and then fill out the form. After you select the amount you want to deposit each month, fill in your recipient's Apple ID and password.

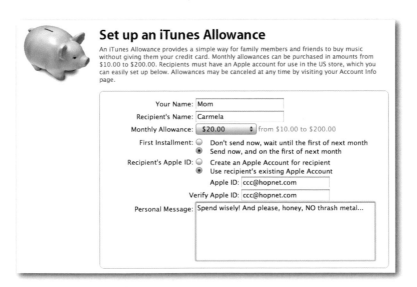

Set up an iTunes Allowance

An iTunes Allowance provides a simple way for family members and friends to buy music without giving them your credit card. Monthly allowances can be purchased in amounts from $10.00 to $200.00. Recipients must have an Apple account for use in the US store, which you can easily set up below. Allowances may be canceled at any time by visiting your Account Info page.

Your Name:	Mom
Recipient's Name:	Carmela
Monthly Allowance:	$20.00 from $10.00 to $200.00
First Installment:	○ Don't send now, wait until the first of next month ● Send now, and on the first of next month
Recipient's Apple ID:	○ Create an Apple Account for recipient ● Use recipient's existing Apple Account
Apple ID:	ccc@hopnet.com
Verify Apple ID:	ccc@hopnet.com
Personal Message:	Spend wisely! And please, honey, NO thrash metal...

Once the giftee logs into the designated Apple Account, she can begin spending—no credit card required. Once the allowance amount has been spent, that's it for music until the following month. (Of course, if the recipient has a credit card on file, she can always put the difference on the card.) If you need to cancel an allowance account, click the Account link on the Store's main page to take care of the matter.

Making an iTunes Wish List

With no paper money flying about to remind you of reality, it's easy to rack up hefty credit card charges. Consider, then, making an iTunes *wish list* to help keep track of songs you want to buy...when your budget is ready.

Making an iTunes wish list is basically just like making any ol' playlist, except you populate it with 30-second song previews from the iTunes Store—complete with their Buy Song buttons that take you right back to the store once you're ready to shop again.

❶ Make a new playlist in iTunes—"Wish List" is a good name.

❷ In the iTunes Source list, click the Store icon.

❸ Shop around the store and drag songs into the new playlist.

If you decide that, in retrospect, you really don't need the 12-inch remix of the Village People's "Macho Man," just click the unwanted track and press Delete.

> **Tip** Tired of scrolling down to the bottom of iTunes to get to your wish list? (That often happens when you've loaded iTunes with playlists, which get listed alphabetically.) Slap an "@" sign at the beginning of the playlist name—@*Wish List*—and your list pops to the top of the Playlist area.

What to Do If Your Download Gets Interrupted

It's bound to happen sometime: You're breathlessly downloading a hot new album or movie from iTunes and the computer freezes, crashes, or your Internet connection goes on the fritz.

If this happens to you, don't worry. Even if your computer crashes or you get knocked offline while you're downloading your purchases, iTunes is designed to pick up where it left off. Just restart the program and reconnect to the Internet.

If, for some reason, iTunes doesn't go back to whatever it was downloading before the incident, choose Store→Check for Purchases to resume your downloading business.

Tip If you need help from a human at Apple you can either call (800) 275-2273 or email them. From the iTunes Store's main page, click the Support link. Your Web browser presents you with the main iTunes service and support page; click any link in the Customer Service area and then, at the bottom of the page that appears, fill out the Email Support form.

The Purchased Playlist

You can find your new songs and videos by clicking the Purchased playlist in the iTunes Source list. You can work with the Purchased playlist as though it were any other playlist. That is, even if you delete a track from it, the song itself still remains in your iTunes library. And behind the scenes, the corresponding music file stays in your My Music→iTunes→iTunes Music (Home→Music→iTunes→iTunes Music) folder.

If you're going to back up anything in your iTunes library, make it the Purchased list. After all, you paid for everything on it and if your hard drive goes south, that particular financial investment is toast. Lucky for you, iTunes 7 and later has a built-in backup tool that can archive copies of all the files you bought from the iTunes Store.

There's more information about backing up in Chapter 3, but if you're in a hurry, choose File→Back Up to Disc. A box pops up to walk you through the process; make sure you have a stack of recordable CDs or DVDs handy.

Setting Up Parental Controls for the Store

If you have children with their own Allowance Accounts, you may not want them wandering around the iTunes Store and buying just *anything*. With the Parental Controls feature, you can still give your children the freedom to spend and discover, but you can restrict the types of things they buy—without having to hover over them every time they click a Store link.

❶ In the iTunes Preferences box (Ctrl+comma/⌘-comma) click the Parental Control tab.

❷ A box unfurls with all the things you can choose to limit. For Store material, you can block songs and other items tagged with the Explicit label, restrict movie purchases to a maximum rating (G, PG, PG-13, or R), and choose the highest TV Show content rating allowable for kids (TV-Y, TV-Y7, TV-G, TV-PG, TV-14, or the mature TV-MA).

❸ Click the lock to password protect the settings box so the kids can't change it themselves.

You can also block certain icons from appearing in the iTunes Source list, including Podcasts, Internet Radio, Shared Music, or even the iTunes Store itself.

Authorizing Your Computer for iTunes Purchases

You can play Store-bought songs and videos only on an *authorized* computer. Authorization is Apple's copy-protection system.

Between work, home, and the family network, not everyone spends time on just one computer these days. So Apple lets you play your Store purchases on up to five computers: Macs, PCs, or any combination. You just need to type in your Apple user name and password on each computer to authorize it to play any songs, videos, or audio books purchased with that account. Each computer must have an Internet connection to relay the information back to Store headquarters. (And don't worry—you don't have to authorize each and every purchase because you authorize the computer to play *all* the items bought from an account.)

You authorized your first machine when you initially signed up for an Apple Account. To authorize another computer:

❶ **On the computer you used to purchase an iTunes Store item, grab any file you've bought from iTunes.** You can drag the files right out of your iTunes window onto your desktop. You can also find all the song and video files in your iTunes Music folder: My Documents→My Music→ iTunes→iTunes Music (Home→Music→iTunes→iTunes Music). Store files are easily recognizable by their *.m4p* or *.m4v* file extensions. Movies are stored in a folder called Movies; TV shows are stored in folders named after the show.

❷ **Move the file to the second computer.** Copy the file onto a CD or USB drive, email it to yourself, transfer it across the network, or use whatever method you prefer for schlepping files between machines.

❸ **Deposit the file in the iTunes Music folder on the second computer. Then, import the copied file into iTunes on the second computer.** To import the file, you can either choose File→Add to Library (and then select and open the file), or just drag the file right into the iTunes window.

❹ **In your iTunes list, select a transferred file and click the Play button.** iTunes asks for your Apple Account user name and password.

❺ **Type your Apple ID and password, and click OK.** This second computer is now authorized to play that file—and any other songs or files you bought using the same Apple Account.

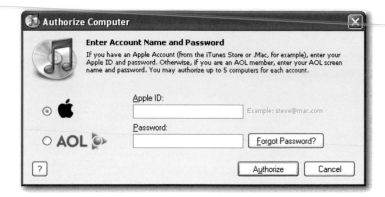

Another way of authorizing a computer before you transfer anything is to choose Store→Authorize Computer.

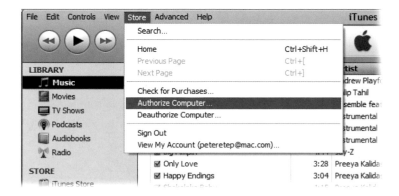

Deauthorizing Your Computer

You won't be able to play purchased music on a sixth computer if you try to authorize it. Apple's authorization system will see five other computers already on its list and deny your request. That's a drag, but copy protection is copy protection.

That means you have to deauthorize another computer if you want to play protected files on Number 6. To deauthorize a computer, choose Store→Deauthorize Computer, and then type in your Apple Account user name and password. The updated information zips back to Apple.

Are you thinking of putting that older computer up for sale? Before wiping the drive clean and sending it on its way, be sure to deauthorize it, so your new machine will be able to play copy-protected files. Erasing a hard drive, by itself, doesn't deauthorize a computer.

If you forget to deauthorize a machine before getting rid of it, you can still knock it off your List of Five, but you have to reauthorize every machine in your iTunes arsenal all over again. To make it so, in the iTunes Store, click the Account link. On the Apple Account Information page, click the Deauthorize All button.

Using Your iPod to Copy Purchases to Other Computers

You may love the convenience of buying music and movies from any Internet-connected Mac or PC—whether it's your regular computer or not. But what do you do if you buy Store stuff on a different computer and need an easy way to move it back to your main machine?

Sure, you can move the files as described a few pages earlier. But that's a hassle. If you have an iPod set to manually manage songs and playlists (Chapter 1), though, you can just use that iPod to ferry Store purchases back to your regular computer. Both computers involved need to be authorized with the same account, but if you're just toting tunes around between your work and home PCs, that shouldn't be a problem. Here's what you do:

❶ Connect the iPod to Computer #1 and load it up with the Store files you want to transfer.

❷ Eject the iPod from Computer #1 and connect it to Computer #2.

❸ In iTunes, choose File→Transfer Purchases From iPod.

This transfer technique works only on Store-bought items, so you can't use it to, say, copy the player's entire library onto another computer since that would involve all sorts of copyright problems.

Seeing Your iTunes Purchase History and Getting iTunes Store Help

The iTunes Store keeps track of what you buy and when you buy it. If you think your credit card was wrongly charged, or if you suspect that one of the kids knows your password and is sneaking in forbidden downloads, you can contact the Store or check your account's purchase history page to see what's been downloaded in your name.

Purchase History
Latest Purchase

🔒 Secure Connection

Date: 10/12/06 10:24 AM
Order: M28872119

Item	Artist	Type	Price
The Saga Begins	"Weird Al" Yankovic	Video	$1.99
The Littlest Birds	The Be Good Tanyas	Video	$1.99
Battlestar Galactica: The Story So Far	Battlestar Galactica	Video	Free
Alabama	U.S. of ANT	Video	$1.99
The Titan On the Tracks	Bones	Video	Free

Subtotal: $5.97
Tax: $0.00
Credit Card Total: $5.97

To do the latter, on the iTunes Store's main page, click the Account link and then click Purchase History. If you have a problem with your bill, or want to submit a specific query or comment, the online help center awaits. From the iTunes Store's main page, click the Support link. Your Web browser presents you with the main iTunes service and support page; click the link that best describes what you want to learn or complain about. For billing or credit card issues, click Billing Support.

 Note The iTunes Store sends out invoices by email, but they don't arrive right after you buy a song. You usually get an invoice that groups together all the songs you purchased within a 12-hour period, or for every $20 worth of tunes that you buy.

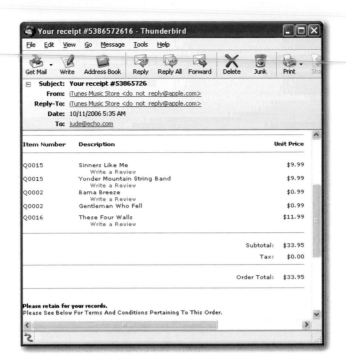

6

Videos Everywhere

In October 2005, a longtime industry rumor came true: Apple finally launched the iPod's video-playing era. All new iPods—that's the standard iPod, not the Nano or Shuffle, mind you—now play video on their gorgeous color screens.

You're not stuck just watching two- or three-minute music video clips, either. As explained in the previous chapter, the iTunes Store has all kinds of cinematic things to buy: full-length Hollywood movies, episodes (or entire seasons) of certain TV shows, and yes, thousands of music videos, just like the kind MTV used to play back when it showcased videos.

This chapter shows you where to find video files and how to juggle them between computer and iPod—as well as how to convert your own digital movies for screening on your own Shirt Pocket Cinema.

Adding Videos to iTunes

The iTunes Store is chock full of videos you can buy. But sometimes you've got your own flicks you want to add to iTunes. No problem. Just drag the file's icon from your desktop and drop it anywhere in iTunes' main window, or choose File→Add to Library to locate and import your files. Once you get videos into iTunes, you can play

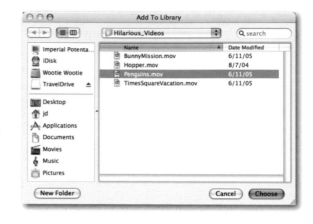

them in iTunes or copy them to your iPod. (Chapter 3 has details.)

Movies and TV shows have their own icons in the Source pane's Library section. Click either one to see a list of items in either category. Music videos are lumped together in a playlist titled "Music Videos."

If you've imported a video yourself and want it to appear in either the Movies or TV Shows section of the Source pane, you may need to tweak the file's labeling info. Open the file's Get Info box (Ctrl+I/⌘-I) and then choose the video format you want from the Video Kind drop-down menu: Movie, Music Video, or TV Show.

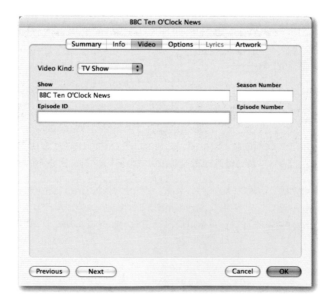

Playing Videos in iTunes

Cranking up your iTunes movie theater is a lot like playing a song: Double-click the title of your chosen video and iTunes starts playing it. When you click either of the right-most two View buttons at the top of the iTunes window (Grouped with Artwork or Cover Flow), you see your videos represented by either a movie-poster type picture or a frame from the video. (Like album covers, video purchases from the iTunes Store come with the nice artwork.)

iTunes gives you a few video-viewing options. You can play the video in the album artwork window (at lower left), opt to have it open in a separate window floating above iTunes, or you can watch it at full-screen size on your computer.

To make your choice, click the General tab on the iTunes Preferences box (Ctrl+comma/ ⌘-comma). Make sure the checkbox next to "Play videos" is turned on and then make your decision with the drop-down menu.

You can also pick a variety of screen sizes under the View menu in iTunes, including Half Size, Actual Size, Double Size, Fit to Screen, and Full Screen.

Transferring Videos to the iPod

Chapter 3 gives you the lowdown on syncing all kinds of files between iTunes and your trusty iPod. If you don't feel like flipping back there, here's a quick summary:

- **Automatic synchronization.** Connect your iPod to the computer and click its icon in iTunes. Click the Movies tab and turn on the "Sync movies" checkbox. You can also choose to sync only certain movies to save space on your iPod. If you have TV programs in your iTunes library, click the TV Shows tab and adjust your syncing preferences there.

- **Manual management.** Click the appropriate library in the Source list (Movies or TV Shows), and then drag the desired files from the main iTunes window onto the icon of your connected iPod.

If you've made any video playlists in iTunes, you can copy those over to the iPod just like you do with music playlists. In case you haven't tried it, making a video playlist is just like making a music playlist. Chapter 3 has all the details on that, too.

Playing Videos on the iPod

Videos you buy from the iTunes Store (and other iTunes-friendly videos) appear in the Videos menu of your iPod after you copy them onto the device. To watch a music video, TV show, or movie, scroll through the various Video submenus (Video Playlists, Movies, Music Videos, TV Shows, and Video Podcasts; there's also a Video Settings menu that's discussed later in this chapter) until you find something you want to watch.

Say you want to watch something in your TV Shows menu. Select TV Shows from the main Videos menu. The next screen lists all your iPod's TV shows. Scroll to the show you want to watch, select the episode you want, and then press the Play/Pause button to start the show.

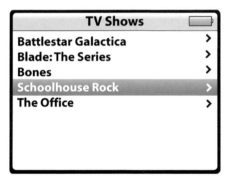
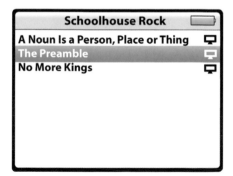

Here are the main iPod playback controls you use when viewing videos:

- **Press the Play/Pause button again to pause the program.** Pausing a video on the iPod works just like hitting Pause on a VCR or TiVo so you can get more Doritos. Press the button again to pick up where you left off.

- **To increase or decrease the video's volume, run your finger along the scroll wheel.** This volume adjustment feature works just like it does when controlling sound levels on songs.

- **To fast-forward or rewind through part of a video, tap the Select button.** A time code bar appears along the bottom of the screen. Use the scroll wheel to advance or retreat through a big chunk of the video. For moving forward and backward in smaller increments, hold down the Fast-Forward and Rewind buttons on the click wheel.

When your video ends, the iPod flips you back to the menu you were last on before you started watching your show. If you want to bail out before the movie's over, press the Menu button.

Some video files come in a letterbox format that creates a thin, horizontal strip of picture across your iPod's display. If you're not into widescreen HamsterVision, visit the Video Settings area of the iPod's Videos menu and change the Widescreen option to Off.

> **Tip** Want your video file to remember its position when you pause or stop it? Easy. In iTunes, select the video and then press Ctrl+I (⌘-I). Click the Option tab and turn on the checkbox next to "Remember playback position."

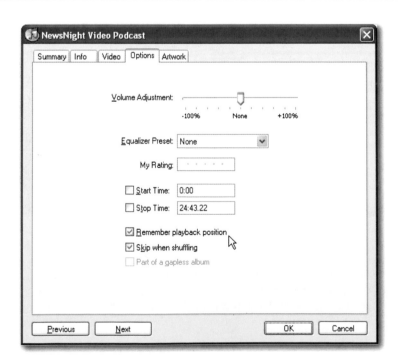

Video Formats That Work on the iPod

As described in Chapter 5, the iTunes Store now sells movies, music videos, and TV shows. You can also import into iTunes your own home movies, downloaded movie trailers, and other bits of video, as long as the files are in QuickTime-friendly video formats.

Compatible video formats include QuickTime Movie and MPEG-4 and have one of these file extensions at the end of its name: *.mov*, *.m4v*, or *.mp4*. Other common video formats like *.avi* or Windows Media Video (*.wmv*) won't play in iTunes, but you can always convert them with Apple's $30 QuickTime software or any of the dozens of video-conversion programs floating around the Web. For more conversion tips, read on—this chapter's loaded with advice.

 Note QuickTime 7, required for watching videos in iTunes, uses new video compression technology called *H.264* to squeeze a whole lotta near-DVD-quality picture into a relatively small file size, giving videos a sharper image and more definition onscreen. The videos you buy from the iTunes Store are encoded with H.264 (also known by its more formal name, MPEG-4, Part 10) and come in a resolution of 640 x 480 pixels—which makes for very nice video, indeed.

Finding iPod-Friendly Videos Online

When Apple rolled out the new video iPods, it made sure to serve up some video *content* for folks to play on the newfangled devices. As explained in Chapter 5, the iTunes Store now sells music videos, classic Pixar cartoons, and selected television shows, all for about $2 apiece, plus full-length Hollywood flicks for $10 to $15 a movie. The Store also hosts a collection of video podcasts for download.

But as everyone knows, the Web is teeming with videos that will never see the bright lights of the iTunes Store. So grab your popcorn and start surfing. Here are a handful of places to find iPod-ready videos to download:

- **Google Video.** Some (not all) of the video clips on the mighty Google site are formatted for the iPod and ready to download. Look for files with a "Download to iPod" button at *http://video.google.com*.

- **Official Movie Web sites.** Many an upcoming film now features a down-loadable trailer formatted just for the iPod. Browse through some of the links at *www.apple.com/trailers* to see what film previews are listed, and then click through to the film's own Web site to see if they offer an iPod download.

- **Veoh.** You can find an eclectic mix of free videos at *www.veoh.com*, in a wide range of categories—and many of them are ready to download to your iPod.

- **Your Own TiVo.** The wily digital video recorder that reads your mind and records your television shows has gotten into the iPod video picture game. The company's TiVoToGo software (which moves recorded shows off the TiVo box and onto Windows computers; no Mac version yet) can also move recorded shows right onto the iPod. Visit *www.tivo.com/4.9.4.1.asp* for more information.

But those aren't the only places to find iPod video. New software and services pop up around the Web all the time, and there are even a few tips and tricks in this chapter for making your own pocket videos.

 Note One of the most popular video-watching sites these days is YouTube (*www.youtube.com*), recently acquired by Google. Unfortunately for iPod fans, the videos on YouTube are *streamed*—broadcast rather than downloaded—which means you have no way to get YouTube's goods onto your iPod.

Video-Conversion Programs for the iPod

A flurry of programs designed to convert all kinds of video files into iPod movies surfaced in the video iPod's wake. In addition to commercial programs, several shareware titles also appeared. Here are a few of each:

- **iVideoToGo.** InterVideo, maker of DVD-copying and playback software, has a $30 conversion program for Windows that converts DVD movies and just about any other video format for iPod compatibility (*www.intervideo.com*).

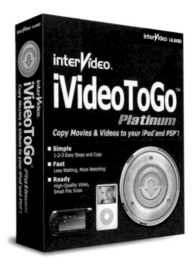

- **PQ DVD to iPod Video Converter**. This $35 program for Windows converts TiVo recordings, DVD video, DiVX, Windows Media Video, RealMedia, and AVI files to the iPod's video format (*www.pqdvd.com*).

- **Videora iPod Converter**. With this freeware, you can gather up all those *.avi* and *.mpg* video clips stashed away on your PC and turn them into iPod video clips. Find it at *www.videora.com*.

- **ViddyUp!** Mac OS X owners can convert their movies, even those in *.avi* and DiVx formats, with this $10 shareware program (*www.splasm.com*).

- **HandBrake.** Mac folks wishing to convert DVD movies and other files for the iPod quickly adopted this easy-to-use bit of freeware (and its faster little sibling, Instant Handbrake). You can get them at *http://handbrake.m0k.org* and various shareware archives around the Web.

If you already use a TV tuner card and your computer's hard drive to record television shows with products like SnapStream's Beyond TV ($150 at *www.snapstream.com*) or Instant TV from ADS Technologies (prices vary; *www.adstech.com*), then you should be able to export and convert these recordings to iPod-ready files with one of the above programs as well. If you're on a Mac, you can use the EyeTV Hybrid for Mac from Elgato Systems ($150 at *www.elgato.com*) and export 320 x 240 MPEG-4 files right from the EyeTV software.

 Note Many DVD owners feel that since they paid for the disc, they own the right to do whatever they want with it, including play it on an iPod. Like commercial compact discs, many people feel that copying DVD movies falls under the fair-use rights consumers are entitled to if they legally purchase the work. Although the movie industry has yet to go after programmers writing DVD decryption and conversion programs with a Napster-style smackdown lawsuit, it may still happen. In any case, if you convert your own commercial DVD movies for use on your iPod, keeping them between you and the iPod is much more ethical than dispensing someone else's copyrighted material on the Internet.

Converting Your Own Home Movies

All those home movies stored on your computer can also find new life on your iPod. Simply export a copy of each file as an MPEG-4 or QuickTime-compatible movie with a screen resolution of 320 x 240 pixels (the size that works best on the iPod). Most popular consumer video-editing programs for Windows, like Pinnacle Studio and Ulead's Video Studio, can export movie files to the MPEG-4 format.

Mac OS X fans who've got iMovie HD can export their film projects right out of that program to the iPod 320 x 240 format from the File menu. To do so, open your finished iMovie project and then:

❶ Choose Share→iPod. The iPod sharing box comes up.

❷ Click the Share button and iMovieHD automatically compresses your selected movie down to size and shuttles a copy right into iTunes, where it's now just a sync away from your iPod.

❸ Get a snack while the program goes to work—the video compression usually takes several minutes.

The process works in a similar manner with other movie-making programs for Windows that offer a conversion tool for making iPod-sized flicks.

Converting Movie Files with iTunes

You can use iTunes 7 and later to convert some videos into an iTunes-friendly format. To do so, add the video to your iTunes library, right-click the track's name, and then, from the shortcut menu, choose "Convert Selection for iPod."

The program grinds away, converting your videos into iTunes-friendly mini-movies that are 320 pixels wide—just the right width for iPodvision. Depending on your computer's power, it may take a while for iTunes to plow through the conversion, but you'll see a progress bar in the status display window giving you an idea of how much farther the program has to go.

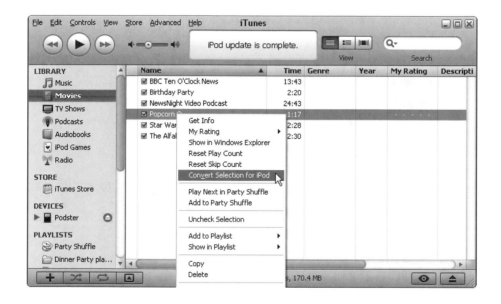

If you have a copy of QuickTime 7 Pro on your computer, there's also a menu option for iPod export. Just open the movie you want to convert with QuickTime 7 Pro, and then choose File→Export and select "Move to iPod" from the menu in the Export box.

Playing iTunes and iPod Videos on Your TV

Movies on the iPod and computer screen are great, but watching them on a bigger screen is often even more relaxing. In case you were wondering, you *can* watch all those movies and other videos on your big TV screen—you just need to connect the computer or iPod to the television.

Here are some ways to turn little movies into big movies:

- Computers with S-video connections can connect to the TV with an S-video cable to play iTunes videos. For the audio, a $10 Y-shaped cable with a stereo mini-plug on one end and the red and white RCA plugs on the other provide the sound.

- If you have a computer-friendly television (the kind that can double as a computer monitor thanks to VGA or DVI ports), you can just plug your laptop right into the TV.

- You can connect the iPod to the TV with a special cable like the Apple iPod AV Cable, shown here, available at *http://store.apple.com* and other places. This $19 cable has a stereo mini-plug on one end for the iPod's headphones jack, and red, white, and yellow RCA plugs on the other end for carrying the audio and video signal to the TV. (Some similar cam-corder cables may also work.)

- If you want a complete solution in one box, try the Apple iPod AV Connection Kit (also in Apple's online store and in stores that sell iPod gear). The kits costs $99, but you get all the cables you need for power and AV connections, plus a Universal Dock to keep your iPod upright and a remote control to let you control the player from across the room.

Once you connect your iPod to the television set, you need to tell it to show the video picture on the big screen; choose iPod→Video→Video Settings and turn the TV Out to "On" by selecting it and pressing the center button.

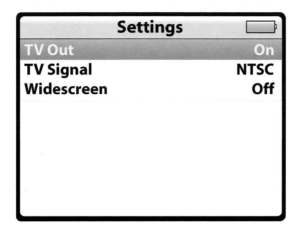

The two other preferences in the Video Settings let you pick a TV Signal (choose NTSC if you live in the U.S. or Japan, or pick PAL if you're connecting to a European or Australian TV set), and opt for the Widescreen letterbox view.

Once you get the iPod or computer hooked up to play movies, be sure to select the alternate video source on your television set, just as you would to play a DVD or game.

Burning Your Video Collection to DVD

Don't get too excited: You can burn your iTunes Store movies, music videos, television shows and other itty bitty videos to a recordable DVD, but you can't actually *play* that disc in your living room DVD player. The DVD burning you do here is only for backing up your files.

Some movie download services like Movielink and CinemaNow let customers buy a download and burn that file to a playable DVD (which is a lot more convenient than schlepping out to Blockbuster on a dark and stormy night). Maybe the iTunes Store will allow that down the road but for now, it's Backup Only.

If you don't remember the steps from Chapter 4 explaining how to back up your files to a disc, here's the highlight reel:

❶ In iTunes, select the video playlist you want to back up (or just jump to Step 2 and back up your whole Purchased playlist or entire iTunes library).

❷ Choose File→Back Up to Disc.

❸ Feed your computer as many recordable or rewritable DVDs as it wants during the process.

When iTunes is done, store the discs in a safe place.

7

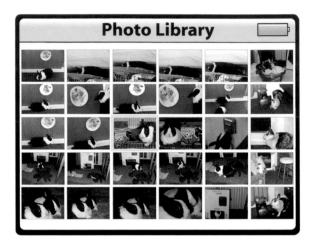

Photo Library

Picturing Your Photos on the iPod

Who needs an overstuffed wallet with cracked plastic picture sleeves to show off your snaps? If you have an iPod or iPod Nano, you can quickly dump all your favorite shots from popular photo programs like Photoshop Elements or iPhoto right onto the iPod and view them on the iPod's glossy color screen. (And even if you don't use a photo program, you just need to tell the iPod where to harvest the pictures on your computer.)

The picture-perfect fun doesn't stop there, either. Both the regular iPod and the Nano can also display your photos in mini-slideshow form, right in the palm of your hand. And if you have the full-sized iPod, you can plug it into the television set with a special AV cable and fire up those slideshows on the living-room screen. This chapter shows you how to do everything except microwave the popcorn for the big show.

What You Need to Put Photos on Your iPod

In addition to a computer loaded with iTunes and an iPod with a color screen, you need a few other things to move pictures to 'Pod:

- **Compatible photo-organizing software for the Mac or Windows—or a folder of photos on your hard drive.** The iPod and Nano can sync with several popular photo programs that you may already have. On the Mac, there's iPhoto 4.0.3 or later. Windows mavens can grab pictures from Adobe Photoshop Album or the more versatile Adobe Photoshop Elements. You can also transfer pictures from a folder of photos on your computer, like the iPhoto Library folder for those who are a few iPhoto versions behind, or My Pictures on the Windows side of the fence.

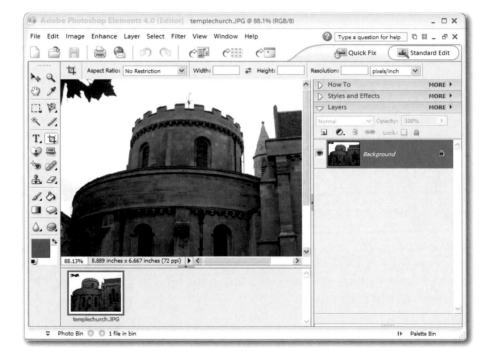

- **Digital photographs in the proper format.** Most of the common photo formats used by digital cameras, Web pages, and email programs are acceptable to iTunes, along with a few others. On the Mac, you can use JPG and GIF files, as well as images in the PICT, TIFF, BMP, PNG, JPG2000, SGI, and PSD formats. In Windows, JPG, GIF, TIF, BMP, PSD, SGI, and PNG files work for the iPod.

You should remember a few other things when adding images to your iPod. For one, you can't import pictures off one of those photo CDs from the drugstore or a backup disc you made yourself—iTunes needs to pull the photos directly from your hard drive. Photos stored on DVDs or CDs won't cut it.

The iPod allies itself with one computer when it comes to photos. Unlike manual music management, where you can grab songs from several different computers and drag them onto your iPod yourself, synchronizing pictures can happen only between one iPod and one computer. If you want to load photos from a different computer, all the photos currently on the iPod will be replaced with ones from the new machine.

You also can't dump photos directly into the iPod from your digital camera—you need to go through iTunes, unless you have a gadget like the iPod Camera Connector (available for $29 at *http://store.apple.com*) that can siphon photos from the camera's memory card over to the iPod's hard drive. These devices don't work with the iPod Nano, though.

Getting Pictures onto the iPod

Okay, so you've got the right iPod and a bunch of pictures in iTunes-friendly formats on your hard drive. How do those photos get from your hard drive to the iPod? They get there like the music does—through iTunes.

But first, you should set up your iTunes and iPod preferences to copy the photos you want to carry around, like so:

❶ Connect the iPod to your Mac or PC with its USB cable.

❷ Once the iPod shows up in the iTunes Source list, click its icon to select it.

❸ On the iPod's preference screen, which appears in the middle of iTunes, click the Photos tab.

❹ Turn on the checkbox next to "Sync photos from" and choose your photo program or folder of choice so iTunes knows where to look for your photos. You can choose to copy over everything or just selected *albums* (sets of pictures).

❺ Click Apply when you've made your selections.

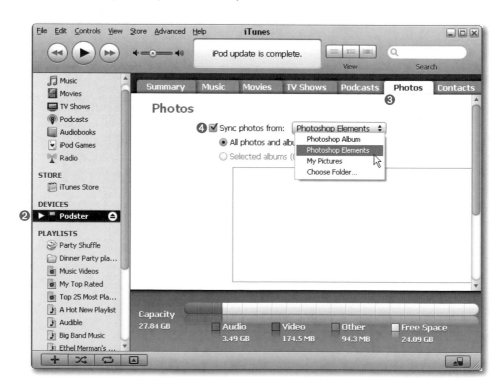

If you don't use any of the programs listed in the "Sync photos from" menu, and just want to copy over a folder of photos on your hard drive, select "Choose folder" from the pop-up menu and then navigate to the desired folder. You can sync just the photos in your chosen folder, or include the photos tucked away in folders *inside* your chosen folder, too.

Select the "All photos and albums" option if you want every single image in your photo program's library to get hauled over to the iPod. (If you don't want those bachelorette-party snaps to get copied, opt for "Selected albums" and choose only the collections you want from your photo program.)

Now, whenever you connect the iPod, it syncs the photo groups you've designated and also picks up any new pictures you've added since you last connected it. During the process, iTunes displays an "Optimizing photos..." message.

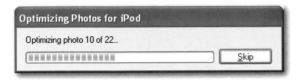

Don't let the term "optimizing" scare you: iTunes hasn't taken it upon itself to touch up your photographic efforts. The program is simply creating versions of your pictures that look good on anything from your tiny iPod screen to your TV screen. Then it tucks away these copies on your hard drive before adding them to the iPod.

Digital Photographer Alert: Storing Full-Quality Photos on the iPod

When iTunes optimizes your photos for iPoddification, it streamlines the images a bit for faster travel instead of copying the big, full-resolution files. But if you want, you can copy the full-size photo files to transfer them to another computer—good news if you're a photographer and you want to haul around a big, print-ready photo collection.

Just follow these steps:

❶ Connect the iPod and select it in the iTunes Source list. Make sure you've set up the iPod as a portable hard drive. (See Chapter 8 for details.) The short version: in your iPod's settings page in iTunes, click the Summary tab and then turn on the "Enable disk use" checkbox.

❷ Click the Photos tab in the iTunes window.

❸ Turn on the "Include full-resolution photos" checkbox.

After you sync, full-resolution copies of the photos sit happily in the Photos folder on the iPod's hard drive. (The Photos folder also has a subfolder called Thumbs that's full of iPod-optimized images all scrunched up in special *.ithmb* files; you can safely ignore these.)

Viewing Pictures on the iPod

Once you've got those photos freed from the confines of your computer, you'll probably want to show them off to your pals. To get to the goods, choose Photos→Photo Library from the iPod's main screen. Or, if you opted for different photo albums when you set up your synchronization preferences, scroll to the name of the album you want to view and press the round center button.

The iPod pops up a screen filled with tiny versions of the pictures in the group you just selected. Use the scroll wheel to maneuver the little yellow highlight box, and then zoom along the rows until you get to the picture you want to see. If you have hundreds of pee-wee pix to plow through, tap the Previous and Next buttons to advance or retreat by the screenful.

Here are some other navigational tips:

- Highlight the photo and press the center button to call up a larger version that fills the iPod screen.

- Press the Previous and Next buttons or the click wheel to move forward or backward through pictures in an album.

- Press the Menu button to go back to the screen of tiny photos.

Playing Slideshows on the iPod

A photo slideshow takes all the click work out of your hands and frees you to admire the pictures without distraction. To run a slideshow on the iPod itself, you need to set up a few things, like how long each photo displays and what music accompanies your trip to Disneyland.

Start by choosing Photos→Slideshow Settings. You'll see a slew of options to shape your slideshow experience.

- Use the Time Per Slide menu to set the amount of time each photo is displayed on screen, from 2 to 20 seconds. You can also choose to move to each new image manually with a tap of the click wheel.

- Use the Music menu to pick one of your iPod's playlists to serve as a soundtrack for your slideshow, if you want one. You may even want to compose a playlist in iTunes just to use with a particular slideshow. If you've already got music assigned to the photo album in iPhoto, choose the From iPhoto option at the top of the menu.

- As with your music, you can repeat and shuffle the order of your photos. You can also add fancy Hollywood-style scene transitions by choosing Photos→Slideshow Settings→Transitions. Pick from several dramatic photo-changing styles, including "Push across" and "Wipe from center."

- To make sure the slideshow appears on the iPod's screen, set the TV Out setting (toward the bottom of the screen) to Off, which keeps the signal in the iPod. (Nano owners don't have to worry about this step.) Or you can select Ask, so that each time you start a slideshow, the iPod politely inquires whether you intend to run your photos on the big or small screen.

Once you've got your settings just the way you want them, select the album or photo you want to start with, and then press the Play/Pause button on the click wheel to start the show. Press the Play/Pause button again to temporarily stop the show; press it again to continue.

Your choice of music, transitions, and time per slide all match what you chose in the Slideshow settings. If you get impatient, you can also use the Previous and Next buttons on the click wheel to manually move things along.

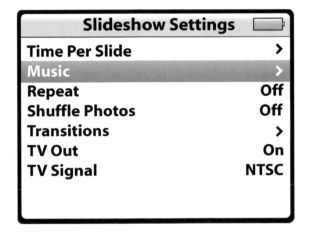

Playing Slideshows on a TV

Flip back to the previous chapter if you need help connecting your iPod to the television set so you can display videos and photos on the TV. These figures show one possible setup. Once you've linked your color screen iPod to your TV, you're almost ready to start the show. You just need to adjust a few more things on the iPod:

❶ **Choose Photos→Slideshow Settings→TV Out→On.** The On option tells the iPod to send the slideshow out to the TV screen instead of playing it on its own screen. (You can also set it to Ask, if you want the iPod to pester you about what screen to use when the time comes.)

❷ **Select your local television broadcast standard.** If you're in North America or Japan, choose Photos→Slideshow Settings→TV Signal→NTSC. If you're in Europe or Australia, choose Photos→Slideshow Settings→TV Signal→PAL. If you're in an area not listed above, check your television's manual to see what standard it uses or search the Web for "world television standards."

❸ **Turn on your TV and select the video input source for the iPod.** You select the input for the iPod's signal the same way you tell your TV to show the signal from the DVD player or VCR. Typically, you press the Input or Display button on your TV's remote to change from the live TV signal to the new video source.

Now, cue up a slideshow on the iPod and press the Play/Pause button. Your glorious photographs—scored to the sounds of your selected music, if you wish—appear on your television screen. (Because television screens are horizontal displays, vertical shots end up with black bars along the sides.)

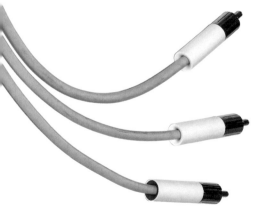

Your preselected slideshow settings control the show, or you can advance it manually with your thumb on the click wheel. Although just one photo at a time appears on the TV screen, if you're driving the iPod, you can see not only the current picture, but the one before it and the one after, letting you narrate your show with professional smoothness: "OK, this is Shalimar *before* we had to get her fur shaved off after the syrup incident…"

If you're showing a video, select the file you want to display on the TV from your Videos menu, and then press Play/Pause.

8

Other Stuff the iPod Can Do for You

The early chapters in this book are all about showing how your iPod works and how to fill it up with music, movies, photos, and more. But if you think that's *all* the iPod can do, think again. That gorgeous color screen is happy to display a copy of your computer's address book, weekly calendar, and helpful text files like your grocery list. If you're looking for a handsome timepiece, the iPod can function as a world clock when you're on the road and as a stop watch when you're on the track.

And regardless of whether you've got a Nano, a Shuffle, or a standard iPod, all models can serve as external hard drives for hauling around monster files like PowerPoint presentations or quarterly reports between computers. So if you've mastered the iPod's AV Club functions and are ready for new challenges, this chapter shows you even more ways to use your iPod.

Using Your iPod as an Address Book

Putting a copy of your contacts file—also known as your computer's address book—onto your iPod is quite easy, as long as you're using recent software. Windows people need to have their contacts stored in Outlook Express, Outlook 2003, or the Windows Address Book (used by Outlook Express and some other email programs). Mac folks need to be using at least Mac OS X 10.4 (Tiger) and the Mac OS X Address Book (shown here), which Apple's Mail program uses to stash addresses in.

To turn your iPod into your little black book, follow these steps:

❶ Connect the iPod to the computer and click its icon when it shows up in the Source list.

❷ In the main part of the iTunes window, click the Contacts tab.

❸ Windows owners: Turn on the checkbox next to "Sync contacts from" and then use the pop-up menu to choose the program you want to copy contacts from. Mac owners: turn on the "Sync Address Book contacts" checkbox. If you've created any contact groups, select them from the "Selected groups" box.

❹ Click the Apply button in the lower-right corner of the iTunes window.

The iPod updates itself with the contact information stored in your address book. If you add new contacts while the iPod is plugged in, choose File→ Update iPod to manually move the new data over to your pocket player. When you decide someone doesn't deserve to be in your contacts anymore and you delete them from your computer's address book, the person will disappear from your iPod the next time you sync it to the computer.

 Note If you use Mac OS X 10.3.9. (Panther), you can sync your Mac OS X Address Book contacts, but you need to use a different program. Fire up the iSync program, press ⌘-N to add your connected iPod to the Device list, and then double-click its icon. Finally, turn on the checkboxes for adding contacts—and iCal calendars, if you like.

To look up a name and address on the iPod side, choose iPod→Extras→ Contacts and scroll to the name of the person you want to look up. Press the center button and the address card for that person pops up on your iPod screen.

Using Your iPod as a Calendar

Just as iTunes can pluck contacts off your computer, it can also snag and display a copy of your daily, weekly, or monthly schedule on your iPod—*if* you happen to use Outlook on your PC or iCal on your Mac.

Just like with the Contacts synchronization, you can find the setting for popping a copy of your iCal or Outlook calendar stashed in the iPod's Preferences area:

❶ Connect the iPod to the computer and click its icon when it shows up in the Source list.

❷ In the main part of the iTunes window, click the Contacts tab. Scroll down past Contacts until you get to Calendars.

❸ Turn on the checkbox next to "Sync calendars from Microsoft Outlook" (Windows) or "Sync iCal calendars" (Mac). If you have multiple calendars, select the ones you want to copy to the Pod.

❹ In the lower-right corner of the iTunes window, click the Apply button.

❺ If the iPod doesn't automatically start updating itself with your date book, choose File→Sync iPod.

To look up your schedule on the iPod, choose iPod→Extras→Calendars. Select the name of the calendar you want to examine and press the round center button. A blue and gray grid pops up on screen, with tiny red flags planted on the squares when you have something scheduled for that day.

Use the scroll wheel to dial up the day you need to see and press the center button to see the day's events.

January 2006						
Sun	**Mon**	**Tue**	**Wed**	**Thu**	**Fri**	**Sat**
25	26	27	28	29	30	31
1	2	3	4	5	6	7
8	9	10	11	12	13	14
15	16	17	18	19	20	21
22	23	24	25	26	27	28
29	30	31	1	2	3	4

A few other calendar-keeping tips:

- If you make use of the To Do list function in your preferred calendar program, those action items appear in their own place on the iPod. Choose iPod→Extras→Calendars →To Do.

- The iPod can also pester you when you have a pending appointment in your calendar that's been marked to pop up a reminder. To turn on the portable Nag Alerts, choose iPod→Extras→Calendars→Alarms. You have your choice of Off, Beep, or Silent.

Tracking Time: Your iPod as a Stopwatch

The Stopwatch feature on the iPod and iPod Nano not only clocks your time around the track, it also *keeps* track of your running sessions. To turn your iPod into a stopwatch, choose Extras→Stopwatch→Timer.

The Stopwatch screen displays separate sets of numbers stacked on top of each other. The top number is the total time of the session. The smaller number underneath is the time for the current lap in hours, minutes, seconds, and milliseconds.

The buttons underneath the timer screen are the same controls you find on any stopwatch—Start and Clear. Use the click wheel to highlight the button you want to use and press the iPod's center button to click it. For example, spin around until the Start button on the left side of the screen is highlighted, and then press the center Select button to start the timer. The stopwatch starts counting and changes the Start button to Pause.

Here's a rundown of how the button names change as you start and stop the timer:

- When you press **Start**, the buttons change to Pause and Lap.

- When you click **Pause**, the timer stops counting and the buttons change to Resume and Done.

- When you click **Lap**, you reset the lap timer (the smaller clock underneath the main one).

- When you click **Resume**, the timer restarts and the buttons change back to Pause and Lap.

- When you click **Done**, the stopwatch slides over to the session log screen.

If the Stopwatch screen still shows an old time listed in the counter, slide the click wheel around until the Clear button is highlighted and tap the center button to reset the clock back to 00:00:00.00.

Counting laps

Each time you finish a lap around the track, tap the Lap button to record that lap's time and restart the lap counter to 00:00:00 so it can begin recording the next one.

If you need to take a breather between laps but aren't done with your exercise session, slide the click wheel around until the Pause button is highlighted and tap the center button.

Session logs

The iPod stores logs of your last five workout sessions, deleting older sessions as you record new ones. To review your progress, scroll to Extras→Stopwatch, where there's a list of your past exercise sessions listed by date and time of day recorded.

```
                 Stopwatch                 ▭▯

          Date:    5/17/06
          Time:    6:45 AM

    Total Time:    00:05:44.585
  Shortest Lap:    00:1:43.985
   Longest Lap:    00:02:02.363
   Average Lap:    00:01:54.861

    Lap 1 Time:    00:01:58.237
    Lap 2 Time:    00:01:43.985
    Lap 3 Time:    00:02:02.363
```

Tick-Tock: Your iPod as a World Clock

As discussed back in Chapter 2, all iPods (except the screenless Shuffle) have built-in clocks with a simple alarm feature. But that's *so* last week. The iPod Nano and video iPod let you use multiple clocks, in different time zones and with their own alarms. If you travel frequently, you can simply create a clock for each location instead of constantly fiddling with time zone settings.

The iPod should already have one clock—the one you created when you first set it up and selected your time zone. To add more, go to Extras→Clock→ New Clock (it's always at the bottom of the list), and press the center button to select New Clock. On the next screen, select a world region, like North America, Europe, Africa, or Asia. Some categories on the Region menu are less obvious: Select Atlantic if you live in Iceland or the Azores; choose Pacific if you live in Hawaii, Guam, or Pago Pago.

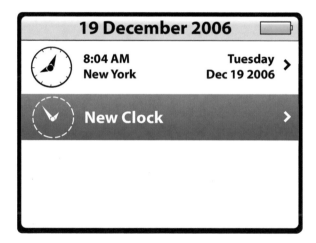

After you select a region, the next screen takes you to a list of major cities and the current time in that part of the world. Scroll and select the town of your choice. Once you pick a city, the iPod creates a clock showing the local time and adds it to your Clock menu.

Adjusting a clock's settings

Each clock you create has its own sublevel of settings you can change. To get to the settings for a specific clock, say, your New York timekeeper, choose Extra→Clock→New York and tap the center button once you get there. The next screen reveals a host of hidden settings, including:

- **Alarm Clock.** See Chapter 2 for instructions on how to set your clock's alarm.

- **Change City.** Choose this option to return to the Region menu, where you can start all over again picking a country and city for this clock to represent.

- **Daylight Savings Time.** The center button is an on/off toggle for Daylight Saving Time (called Summer Time in some parts of the world). For example, you'd set it to On in the summer to keep New York properly represented on your iPod.

- **Delete This Clock.** If you're tired of this town and its time, take it off the menu with this command.

- **Sleep Timer.** The iPod can lull you to sleep and shut itself off automatically. See Chapter 2 for the details.

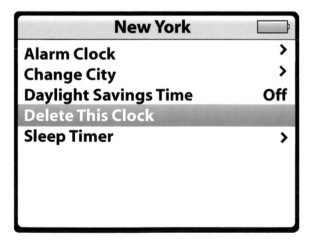

Using Your iPod as a Portable Hard Drive

If being a portable entertainment system and organizer isn't enough, your iPod can also serve as a portable disk to shuttle documents, spreadsheets, presentations, and other files from one computer to another.

To give your iPod these file-toting powers:

❶ Plug your Pod into the computer.

❷ When the iPod icon shows up in the Source list, click it and then click the Summary tab in the main iTunes window.

❸ Turn on the checkbox next to "Enable disk use" in the Options area of the Summary screen. (If you have an iPod Shuffle, use the onscreen slide to designate just how much of your one gigabyte you want to use for music and how much for songs.)

❹ In the lower-right corner of the iTunes window, click the Apply button. If you forget, iTunes reminds you that you modified an iPod setting and prompts you to OK the change.

Keep in mind that once you turn your iPod into an external hard drive, you have to treat it like one by formally ejecting the drive from iTunes before you yank the iPod out of the computer's USB port. Click the Eject

icon next to the iPod's name in the iTunes Source list to safely free it from the computer.

Your iPod now shows up in the My Computer area of Windows or on the Mac desktop. You can drag files on and off the iPod just like you would with any other drive connected to the computer: Drag the files onto the iPod's icon, or double-click the icon and create folders to put your files in. Delete files by dragging them to the Trash or Recycle Bin. Steer clear of the folders labelled Calendars, Contacts, and Photos; the iPod uses them for storage of those items. The next page shows you how to use the Notes folder.

Your music, movies, and other iTunes stuff are kept in a special, invisible place on the iPod, so copying regular computer files onto the iPod doesn't affect them. (And syncing your music with the Mac or PC doesn't affect the computer files, either.) However, remember that the more you fill up your iPod with entertainment, the less room you have to store data files—and vice versa.

 Note A Mac can read a Windows-formatted iPod or iPod Nano, but Windows can't read the Mac disk format. If you want to use your iPod with both systems, plug it into the PC first and let it format itself for Windows. The Shuffle automatically works with both Macs and PCs.

Reading Text Files on Your iPod

The squint factor may be a little high, but the iPod or iPod Nano can also lend its screen for displaying text files, which comes in handy if you want to review class notes while relaxing or skim your talking points before a presentation.

You create iPod Notes from plain text files (with a *.txt* extension) like those from Windows NotePad or TextEdit on a Mac. You can't use full-fledged word-processing documents from Microsoft Word or Apple-Works, unless you save them as plain text files.

To use the iPod's Notes feature:

❶ Connect the iPod to the computer as an external disk. (Flip back two pages to find out how.)

❷ Once you've saved your text files in the proper plain-text format, open the iPod by double-clicking its icon on the Mac desktop or in the My Computer window.

❸ Drag the files into the Notes folder on the iPod.

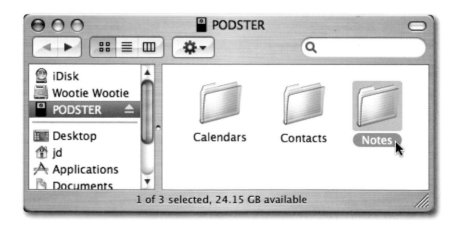

④ After you've copied your text files, eject the iPod from iTunes by clicking the Eject button next to its name in the Source list or using the Eject button in the corner of the iTunes window.

⑤ When you're ready to start reading, choose Extras→Notes. You'll see the names of your text files listed in the Notes menu. Scroll to the one you want and click the iPod's center button to bring it onscreen.

As you read, you can use the scroll wheel to page up and down through the file. Press the Menu button to close the file and return to the list of Notes files. If you can't find a document you're looking for in the Notes menu, open the Notes folder on the iPod and make sure it's indeed a *.txt* file.

Boswell's Life of Johnson.txt

Preface
**In making this abridgement of Boswell's Life of Johnson
I have omitted most of Boswell's criticisms, comments,
and notes, all of Johnson's opinions in legal cases, most
of the letters, and parts of the conversation dealing
with matters which were of greater importance in
Boswell's day than now. I have kept in mind an old habit,
common enough, I dare say, among its devotees, of
opening the book of random, and reading wherever
the eye falls upon a passage of especial interest. All
such passages, I hope, have been retained, and enough
of the whole book to illustrate all the phases of
Johnson's mind and of his time which Boswell observed.**

Using the iPod as a text reader is a handy way to bring along your grocery list so you can rock while you shop. If you want to browse more challenging prose than "Buy Pampers," though, swing by Project Gutenberg's Web site at *www.gutenberg.org*. Here, you can download thousands of public-domain literary works as plain text files and drag them right into your iPod's Notes folder for a little Shakespeare, Schopenhauer, or Sun Tzu.

Recording Audio with Your iPod

With an optional microphone attachment, you can convert your iPod or second-generation iPod Nano into a handheld recorder to capture voice memos, class lectures, interviews, or Big Random Thoughts you may have while on the road.

You can find iPod-friendly microphones in stores that sell iPod gear or online at *www.apple.com/ ipodstore*. The Belkin TuneTalk Stereo Microphone shown here ($70 at *www.belkin.com*) is one example of the products you can find for iPod recordings.

Here's what you do after you buy an iPod-compatible microphone:

❶ Once you have a microphone attached to the iPod, the Voice Memo screen appears on the iPod's screen.

❷ With some mics, you can choose the audio quality of the recording session. Pick "High Quality" to make recordings with the best sound. The tradeoff? These files take up more space on your iPod's disk. Choose "Low Quality" to make smaller files that don't sound as rich but hog less iPod space.

❸ Select Record on the iPod's screen and press the center button to start the session.

❹ Start talking. If you need to pause recording for a minute, use the on-screen Pause option.

❺ When you're done recording, choose Stop and Save.

To find your recordings on the iPod, choose Extras→Voice Memos and select the recording you want—which you'll see listed by time and date. (People who don't have iPod mics won't see the Voice Memos menu item.) Press Play to hear the recording, just like you would a song.

You can copy the voice recordings back to your computer either manually or automatically if your iPod is set to synchronize itself with your Mac or PC. Here's how:

- If you manually manage your iPod's contents or have it configured to use as an external disk, connect it to the computer. Open the iPod's icon from the desktop (Mac) or the My Windows area (Windows). Then open the Recordings folder on the iPod. Drag the time-stamped WAV files onto a folder on your computer, where you can listen to them like any other audio file.

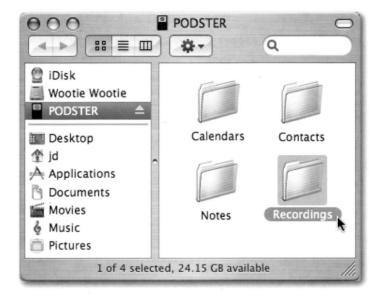

- If you automatically synchronize your iPod, connect it to the computer. Your homemade recordings are copied into a Voice Memos playlist in the iTunes Source list and erased from the Voice Memos area in the iPod's Extras menu. You can find them again on the iPod, however, on the Voice memos *playlist* in the iPod's Music menu.

iPod Out Loud

Now that you've spent all that time getting your iPod fully loaded, you probably want to listen to your playlists, albums, audio books, and podcasts wherever you happen to be—including in the car or on your big booming home stereo system. Who wants to be stuck in traffic listening to low-budget mattress commercials when you can use your car's audio system for cranking up those iPod tunes?

If you can load it onto your iPod, you can channel it through most any sound system—and it's not even that expensive, either. This chapter explains the simple procedures for playing your iPod songs through the woofers and tweeters in your life. (If you want to play iPod movies on your TV, flip back to Chapter 6).

Checklist: Taking Your iPod on the Road

Since the glorious days of crackly AM radio, music and driving have gone hand in hand. These days, a stereo system with an AM/FM radio and a cassette deck is the bare minimum for most cars, and late-model vehicles now cruise around with all sorts of high-end equipment, from MP3-compatible CD players to satellite radio. (Whether the music you can play on them has improved over the years is still subject to debate.)

If having your playlists with you is your idea of paradise by the dashboard light, you have several inexpensive ways to integrate your iPod with your car's stereo system. Whatever method you choose, you have to consider two factors:

- **How to connect your iPod to your existing audio system.** You have your pick of using either a cable or wireless connection.

- **How to power your iPod.** Of course, your iPod can run fine on its battery for short trips. If you're retracing historic Route 66 or barreling down I-95 from Maine to Miami, however, you'll probably want to invest in an adapter that can power your iPod from the car's electrical system.

You've got three main ways to get your iPod piping through the car speakers, some of them more expensive than others. Here are the typical options discussed in detail over the next few pages:

- **Using an FM transmitter.** These inexpensive devices let you borrow an empty frequency from your car's radio and play the iPod's music over the airwaves—no cables snaking across the dashboard required.

The RoadTrip, an FM transmitter and charger, made by Griffin Technology.

The Belkin TuneBaseFM combination charger and FM transmitter.

- **Using a wired adapter.** Another option—especially if your car still has a cassette player—is getting one of those cassette-shaped gadgets that plugs into the tape deck and offers a wire to plug into the iPod's headphones port. Some car stereos also offer an auxiliary jack you can use to plug in your iPod.

- **Using a special iPod aftermarket kit or custom installation.** If you really want fine sound and have the budget for it, several companies now offer special kits that add an iPod-friendly cable to your existing in-dash stereo system.

The popularity of the iPod over the past few years has even led major automobile manufacturers to include iPod cables wired right into their new cars. So if you're in the market for new wheels anyway, why not ask about getting your *click wheel* on the road, too?

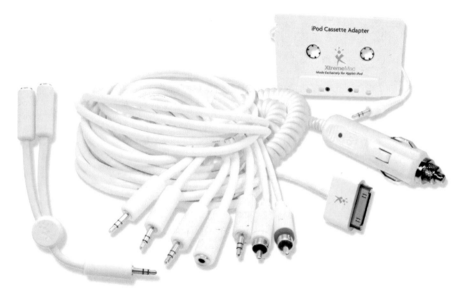

XtremeMac's Audio Kit for iPod gives you a wired adapter, a headphone splitter, and enough cables to hook your iPod up to a car or home stereo.

The FM Connection: Playing Your iPod Through a Radio's Speakers

If you're not a fan of wires, you can buy a doohickey that lets you broadcast your iPod's tunes over any nearby radio (not just your car's). These so-called FM transmitters have their pros and cons. True, you don't have to deal with cables or cords snarling the dashboard and they're fairly inexpensive. But the sound quality can vary—it depends on the strength of the signal—and radio is frustratingly prone to interference (static). If you live in a radio-heavy metropolitan area like New York or Los Angeles, finding a usable empty frequency can be an exercise in frustration.

Still, if you think an FM transmitter is your ticket to ride, you have several choices, among them:

- **iTrip, iTrip Auto, or RoadTrip**. Griffin Technology makes several eye-catching gadgets designed to pump your music from your iPod or Nano through the dashboard. The $50 iTrip plugs into the iPod's dock-connector port to transmit the FM signal and uses the iPod's battery for its juice.

    If you want a built-in charger with your FM frequencies, consider Griffin's iTrip Auto ($70) or RoadTrip ($90) devices, which plug right into your car's cigarette lighter; the RoadTrip also provides a cradle to keep the iPod within easy reach on the dashboard.

    All models are at *www.griffintechnology.com*.

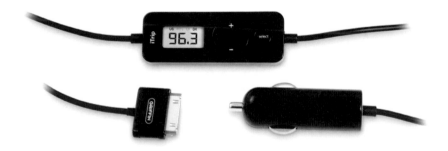

- **The DLO TransPod**. This transmitter also serves as a secure dashboard mount for the iPod. For power, it plugs into the car's cigarette lighter. The TransPod, which works with all recent click wheel-sporting iPods—including the Nano and the video-playing iPod—is available for $100 at *www.dlo.com*, along with other car accessories for iPods.

- **Belkin TuneCast 3 or TuneBaseFM**. Belkin has a whole slew of products to make your iPod loud and proud, including the $50 TuneCast 3 FM transmitter that connects through the headphone port and fits any iPod. If you have an iPod or Nano and a long trip ahead of you, the TuneBase FM ($80) combines a charger and cradle, plus adapters to fit your particular Pod model. You can find all of Belkin's iPod offerings at *www.belkin.com*.

Connecting Your iPod to a Car's Cassette Player

You may prefer to stick with cables, either because the sound quality is better than an FM transmitter or because you can't get a consistently clear signal in your part of FM Land.

One solution is an adapter that resembles an audiocassette. An attached cable and stereo miniplug link the iPod to the car's stereo—if your stereo is equipped with a cassette player, that is. You just plug the cable into the iPod, slip the cassette into the dashboard, and use your iPod just like normal.

Some examples:

- **The Sony CPA-9C Car Connecting Cassette**. The Sony unit is designed for connecting Sony's own portable Discman and MiniDisc players to the car's stereo, but it also works with the iPod and costs less than $5 at *www.amazon.com*.

- **XtremeMac iPod Cassette Adapter**. This cassette adapter fits any iPod model and comes with a gold-tipped miniplug. It's about $20 from *www.xtrememac.com*.

- **Griffin Technology SmartDeck**. Not only does this $30 adapter bring your iPod and cassette deck together to make music though the iPod's dock connector, it also lets you use the forward and reverse buttons on the stereo to advance or retreat through the tracks on your iPod's playlists. The SmartDeck, available at *www.griffintechnology.com*, also enhances the audio quality through the stereo by selecting the optimal volume on the iPod. (Shuffle owners can use Griffin's $15 DirectDeck adapter.)

Incidentally, if your car's stereo console has a 3.5 mm jack on the front as an auxiliary input, you can use a simple male-to-male miniplug audio cable to connect your iPod (under $10 at Radio Shack or audio stores). You can also find this type of cable at places like Monster (*www.monstercable.com*), which in addition to making just about every kind of high-quality audio and video cable, sells the Monster MP3 Connect Portable Audio Player to Car Stereo Cable. Say *that* five times fast.

Some stereo units have the auxiliary jack on the back of the unit, so if you're installing a new stereo in the car, hook up a cable to the auxiliary jack and run it through the dash so it's there for easy RoadPodding, if you ever need it.

iPod and Serious Car Audio Fans: The Custom Installation

Automobile manufacturers and car audio specialists have also fallen under the spell of the iPod's sweet siren song and are even making modifications to accommodate it—if they don't sell models that already include iPod connectivity. Apple has a list of car makers that support iPod connections at *www.apple.com/ipod/carintegration.html* (pictured below), where there's also a link to after-market solutions to retrofit your car's sound system for an iPod connection.

Here are a few other systems to satisfy your mobile iPod audio needs:

- **Alpine iPod Interface KCA-422i.** Alpine Electronics has been develop-
  ing iPod adapters that work with its in-car stereo systems for years, and
  the company's latest solution is the easiet yet. This contraption is a simple
  cable—no bulky interface box needed—that charges the iPod battery
  and displays song information on your car stereo's screen. The Alpine
  iPod Interface KCA-422i costs around $30 and works with a handful of
  the company's source units—the industry name for the dashboard stereo—which start at about $200. The Alpine iPod Interface is compatible
  with dock-connecting iPods and can
  be installed by an Alpine-authorized
  car audio dealer. Check out *www.*
  alpine-usa.com for more information.

- **Monster iCruze for iPod.** Monster Cable comes to the rescue of those
  without a BMW or Alpine Stereo with its $80 iCruze interface box that
  connects the iPod to a factory-installed or aftermarket car stereo. The
  iCruze plugs into the car's satellite
  radio port or CD changer. You can
  call up songs and playlists on the
  connected iPod through the CD
  player controls on the dashboard
  or, in some cars, built into the
  steering wheel. The iCruze and an
  optional LCD display for it are at
  www.monstercable.com.

- **Dension iceLink Plus for iPod.** The Dension iceLink Plus is another
  connection system that brings iPod and car stereo together for high-
  fidelity fun. Once your Pod is strapped in and wired up, you can control
  your playlist navigation through the dashboard and see song information from the iPod on your stereo's display. Not only does the iceLink Plus
  (*www.dension.com/icelinkplus.php*) work with a number of existing stereo
  units in cars from Ford, Chrysler, Honda, Toyota, Subaru, and other manufacturers, it has compatible hardware to cradle most versions of the iPod.
  Prices range from about $200 to $400, depending on your equipment.
  Dension also distributes the DICE iPod integration kit ($160 or so; *www.*
  diceelectronics.com), another system that lets you use your car's existing
  stereo to see your iPod's songs and control your music.

Finding a Power Source for Your iPod

Your car's cigarette lighter can serve a far healthier role than its original purpose, thanks to the fact that it can accommodate an iPod battery charger. You'll live a long, healthy life without ever having to worry about the iPod conking out in the middle of your favorite song when you're on the road. Several companies make these car chargers, including three well-known iPod accessory mavens:

- **PowerJolt.** Sporting a two-tone color scheme, this $20 doodad from Griffin Technology powers Pods on the road. It comes with a four-foot USB cable to string between the PowerJolt and the iPod. It works with most modern dock-connecting iPods, including the Nano; you can find it at *www.griffintechnology.com*.

- **DLO AutoCharger.** This stylish appliance powers your player and recharges it through the car's cigarette lighter, using three color-coded lights that let you keep tabs on your iPod's charging status. The $20 charger comes in either black or white and has a coiled cord that can stretch out to about 5 feet. You can get one at *www.dlo.com*.

- **Xtreme Mac InCharge Traveler**. No matter if you travel by plane, train, or automobile, the InCharge Traveler global charging kit keeps your iPod powered up. This $80 collection of cords and adapters includes a car charger, Empower adapter for commercial airline electrical systems, and regular electrical power adapter that you can use anywhere from an Amtrak train to a Japanese hotel room—plug adapters and voltage converters included. The company also sells a $20 charger just to use in the car; all are at *www.xtrememac.com*.

- **Belkin Auto Kit**. Designed for dock-connecting models, the Belkin Auto Kit includes a cable for charging your iPod from the car's cigarette lighter, plus an audio-out jack and adjustable amplifier that works with Belkin's TuneCast or cassette adapter (neither of which is included) for blasting iPod tunes through the car radio. The kit sells for $40 in the iPod accessories area at *www.belkin.com*.

Connecting the iPod to a Home Entertainment System

CD players that can play discs full of MP3 files cost less than $100. But if you have an iPod, you already have a state-of-the-art MP3 player that can connect to your existing system for under $20—or spend a little more and get the full iPod AV Club experience.

Connecting with an audio cable

To link the iPod to your stereo, you need the right kind of cable and a set of input jacks on the back of your receiver. Most audio systems come with at least one extra set of inputs (after accounting for the CD player, cassette deck, and other common components), so look for an empty AUX jack.

The cable you need is a Y-shaped cord with a 3.5 mm (1/8") stereo miniplug on one end and two bigger RCA plugs at the other end. The stereo miniplug is the standard connector for Walkman-style headphones (and for speakers and microphones); RCA plugs are standard connectors for linking stereo components together.

You plug the smaller end into the iPod's headphones jack, and the RCA plugs into the left and right channel jacks on the back of your stereo. Most online iPod superstores like XtremeMac, Griffin Technology, DLO, and Belkin sell their version of the Y-shaped cable for iPod. There's a list of sites that sell cool iPod stuff at the end of this chapter.

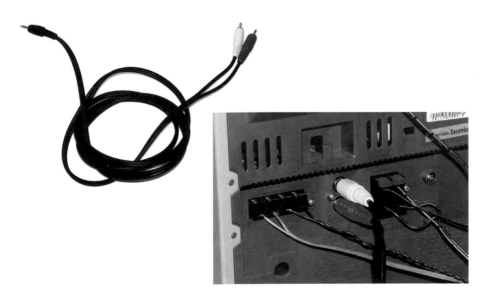

Adding an iPod dock

Once you have your cables, you can also get an iPod dock to connect the player to your entertainment system. The benefit? Most docks come with remotes so you can control your iPod from the couch. The Universal Dock sells for $40 at *http://store.apple.com* and even works with Apple's own miniature white remote control (available for another $30). The U-Dock comes with plastic adapters that serve as little iPod booster seats so the smaller-sized Nano can sit just as securely as a full-sized iPod.

For $100 in Apple's store, you can get Apple' iPod AV Connection Kit, which includes the dock, the remote, the iPod AV cable, a spare USB cable, and an AC power adapter to keep your iPod pumping pictures, videos, and music into your TV and stereo system.

Companies like Kensington and DLO also sell docks to connect the iPod to a stereo system. DLO's HomeDock comes with its own remote control and can pipe your iPod's music, photos, and videos through your home entertainment altar.

Streaming iTunes Music with the AirPort Express

If you have a large iTunes music library and happen to be using an AirPort Express (Apple's portable wireless base station) with your home network, you can merge the two into a streaming music system that beams your computer's music over the wireless network and out through the stereo speakers. If you don't have an AirPort Express, you can buy one for $129 at *http://store. apple.com* and other places.

Setting up an AirPort Express to work with iTunes is a multi-step adventure:

❶ **Plug the AirPort Express into the wall near the stereo.** Be sure to pick an electrical outlet that's within a cable's reach of both your stereo and your broadband modem.

❷ **Plug the Ethernet cable from your broadband modem or router into the AirPort Express.** This brings in the zippy Internet connection from your cable, satellite, or DSL service into your AirPort Express, which then beams it out to all the wirelessly equipped Macs and PCs in the house.

❸ **Connect your stereo system or powered speakers to the AirPort Express.** After you plug the Airport Express into the wall, use a Y-shaped cable (the one with the two RCA plugs on one end and the miniplug on the other, mentioned earlier in this chapter) to connect the AirPort Express to the stereo system or a pair of powered speakers. If your system has a digital Toslink port, you can also use a digital fiber optic cable to connect the two instead. (Speakers that use a USB connection don't work with AirPort Express.)

❹ **Install the AirPort Express software from the CD in the box.** The AirPort Express Assistant program walks you through the network set-up process, automatically picking up your Internet settings and prompting you to name the base station. Naming it something like "Living Room Stereo" is helpful when it comes to using iTunes with the base station.

⑤ **Open iTunes and look for a pop-up menu with the name of your AirPort Express.** Once you start up iTunes with the AirPort Express running, you'll notice a little pop-up menu at the bottom of the iTunes window (circled). One menu item is My Computer and the other is the name of the base station.

With everything connected and turned on, select the base station in the iTunes pop-up menu and click the Play button to blast your playlists out through the stereo.

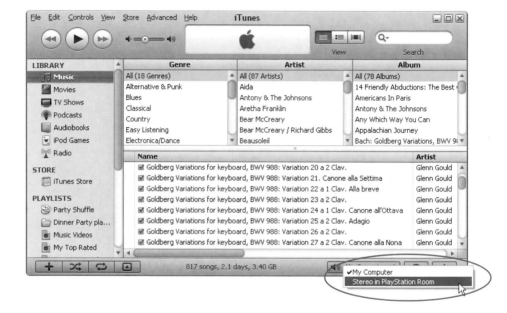

Playing the iPod Through Portable Speakers

You can hook up your iPod to a home audio system to share your sounds, but sometimes it's more convenient to get the iPod a set of speakers to call its own. Some speakers connect to the iPod's headphone jack with a stereo miniplug cable, while others connect to the iPod's dock connector port.

The price and quality of iPod speakers can range from $15 cheap plastic things at the grocery store to $300 systems from high-end audio companies like Bose, JBL, Sony, Tivoli, and others. Here are a few speakers to sample, but check the list at the end of the chapter for more places to find booming iPod accessories.

- **Altec Lansing iPod Speakers.** Portable, self-powered, and supremely Podly, Altec Lansing has a line of speakers that have been letting iPods raise the roof with booming sound for several years. Some of the latest models include the inMotion im500 for the iPod Nano and the M602, which includes a video output port for the regular iPod. When plugged in, most speakers also charge the connected iPod and many models come with remote controls. See the full line of iPod speakers online at *www.alteclansing.com*.

- **DLO iBoom.** Boomboxes may have fallen out of favor, but the iBoom from Digital Lifestyle Outfitters lets you combine your iPod with a four-speaker system that can crank out 20 watts of sound per channel on the boat, beach, or backyard barbecue. The iBoom also includes an FM radio. It runs on six D batteries or its AC power cord and fits dock-connecting iPods, including the Nano. You can find it at *www.dlo.com*.

- **Apple iPod Hi-Fi.** Apple joined the external speaker party in early 2006 with its iPod Hi-Fi, a shoebox-size black-and-white unit with a built-in iPod cradle. It's designed with all the touches you'd expect from the iPod's parent: a click-wheel style remote control, an internal power supply (no clunky power brick to deal with), and an analog and digital optical input jack (good for a nearby radio or CD player or, better yet, an Airport Express to tap into all the iTunes floating around on your home network). The Hi-Fi also has a rear battery compartment if you want to boom this box outside. The Hi-Fi sells for $349 on Apple's site at *http://store.apple.com*.

Where to Find Cool iPod Stuff

Since the iPod's arrival in 2001, its accessories market has been growing by leaps and bounds. There are several online iPod superstores around now with a huge selection of merchandise, from stylish cases to snap-on FM radios. If you want to see what's out there without even having to leave your desk, the bigger Podfocused Web shops include:

- **The Apple Store** (*http://store.apple.com*). Apple has pages and pages of products for all its iPod offspring.

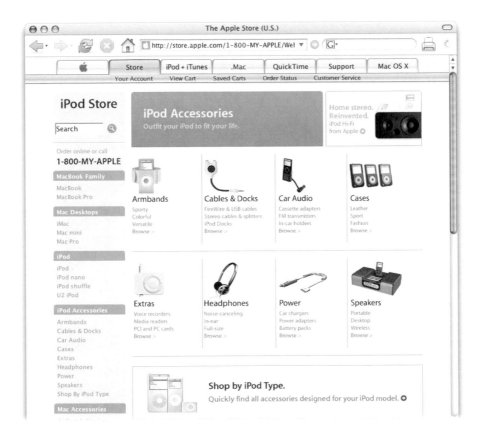

- **XtremeMac** (*www.xtrememac.com*). XtremeMac has an extremely large amount of iPod merchandise. It's notable for its clear plastic MicroShield cases for active iPod video lovers, creative charging solutions, and miles of sleek white audio cables to connect the iPod to car stereos and home audio systems.

- **Digital Lifestyle Outfitters.** (*www.dlo.com/store*). One of the first makers of iPod accessories, DLO makes and sells a wide variety of cases, docks, car chargers, and even the iBoom box. The company also sells its own iPod Care Kit, a three-step cleaning solution to help clear up scratches and scuffs on beloved-but-battered iPods.

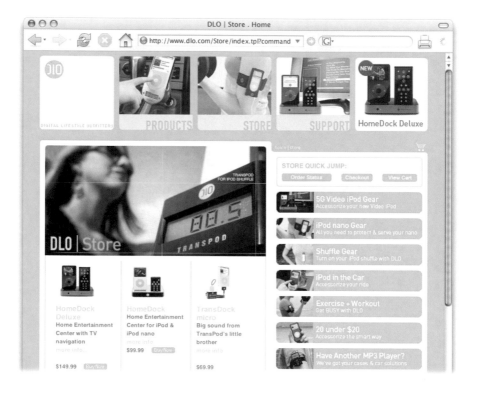

- **Gadget Locker** (*www.thinkdifferentstore.com*). You can find tons of cases, speakers and docks here, plus a CD-ripping service if you don't have the time to get your own music on the iPod.

- **Griffin Technology** (*www.griffintechnology.com*). With its iTrip line of FM transmitters and its crafty SmartDeck (both described in this chapter), Griffin's forte is products that get your iPod thumping through the car and home stereo speakers. The company also sells a handful of cases and items like the RadioShark, which is designed to add broadcast radio to your computer and iPod.

Other companies like Belkin (*www.belkin.com*), Kensington (*www.kensington. com*), and Monster Cable (*www.monstercable.com*) have healthy iPod accessory sections on their sites, especially if you're looking for cables, docks, FM transmitters, and the like.

Computer and electronics stores like CompUSA, Circuit City, and Best Buy usually have a section devoted to iPod cases and speakers. And as a sign of the iPod's mainstream cultural significance, even all-purpose suburban bazaars like Target also include a rack or two of iPod stuff for sale.

10

What to Do When the iPod Isn't Working Right

I t's bound to happen sometime: the iPod locks up, freaks out, or just isn't its usual cheerful self. Luckily, many iPod problems can be solved with a button-tap here, a battery charge there, and your portable Pod Life is back to normal.

Of course, the iPod is a little mini-computer in its own right, and there *are* bigger issues that are more involved or require the help of a technical expert. Figuring out what your iPod is trying to tell you when it's sick is the first step. This chapter explains what to do if your iPod's acting weird—and where to go if you need more information or can't fix it yourself.

Apple's Alphabet: The 5 Rs of iPod Repair

After a few years of dealing with irate iPod owners whose devices were on the fritz, Apple's tech support team came up with a memorable formula designed to fix most iPod/iTunes problems. As posted in the iPod support section of its Web site (*www.apple.com/support/ipod/five_rs*) Apple recommends "The 5 Rs" whenever you encounter trouble: Reset, Retry, Restart, Remove, and Restore.

Here's what each R stands for, along with a few more helpful details:

• **Reset** your iPod, as explained in this chapter.

• **Retry** the connection by plugging the iPod into a different USB port on your computer.

• **Restart** your computer and check for any new software updates you may need to download and install.

• **Reinstall** your iPod and iTunes software with fresh versions downloaded from *www.apple.com/itunes*.

• **Restore** the iPod's software (also explained later in this chapter).

The next few pages cover these steps and more, so you can avoid that sixth, painful R: *Ramming* your head into the wall when your iPod won't work.

Resetting Your iPod

If your iPod seems frozen, confused, or otherwise unresponsive, you can *reset* it without losing your music and data files. Some settings, like Bookmarks in long audio book files and On-The-Go Playlists may not be preserved, but at least you can get things running again with this easy quick fix:

❶ Make sure the battery is charged and then slide the Hold switch on and off again.

❷ Press and hold down the Menu and center Select buttons.

❸ Hold the buttons down until you see the Apple logo appear on the screen. This could take several seconds (but less than 10) to kick in, and you may have to do it twice, but keep pressing until you see the Apple logo.

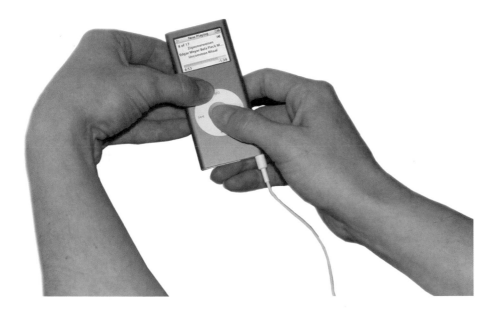

If the technology gods are smiling, the iPod goes through its little start-up sequence and then returns you to the main menu.

A stalled or befuddled iPod Shuffle may also need a good firm reset from time to time, but like the Shuffle itself, resetting it is a bit simpler than wrestling with a regular iPod: Turn the On/Off switch to the Off position, wait five seconds or so, and then flip it back to the On position.

Downloading and Reinstalling iTunes and iTunes Updates

If iTunes is acting up, you may need to download and install a fresh version of the program. The latest version's always waiting at *www.apple.com/itunes/ download*. The program itself may also alert you to a new version—or you can make sure it does in the future:

- If you use iTunes for Windows, choose Edit→ Preferences→General and turn on "Check for updates automatically." If you prefer to check yourself, choose Help→Check for Updates.

- The Mac's Software Update program is designed to alert you, via a pop-up dialog box, about new updates for iTunes. If you've turned Software Update off (in System Preferences), however, you can run it manually by choosing Software Update from the Apple menu.

As with any software update, once you download the software, double-click the installer file's icon and follow along as the program takes you through several screens of upgrade excitement.

If you're reinstalling the same version of the program, the iTunes installer may ask if you want to either *Repair* or *Remove* the software. Choosing Repair can often fix damaged files or data iTunes needs to run properly. It can also be a quicker fix than fully removing the program and reinstalling it all over again.

Using the Diagnostics Tools in iTunes for Windows

With different PC hardware manufacturers out there and multiple versions of Windows in the mix, the PC side of the iTunes/iPod fence can be a little unpredictable. To help sort things out, iTunes 7 for Windows includes a new feature called Diagnostics, which can help troubleshoot three categories of woes. Your choices include:

- **Network Diagnostics.** These tests check your computer's Internet connection and its ability to access the iTunes Store.

- **iPod Diagnostics.** These diagnostics don't actually test the iPod's own hardware or software, but they do examine the way your PC connects to your iPod.

- **CD/DVD Diagnostics.** If you're having trouble getting music to import into iTunes from a CD—or can't burn your own discs, these tests inspect your PC's disc drive for problems and incompatibilities.

To run the tests, choose Help→ Run Diagnostics, select a category and then follow along onscreen. Each diagnostic program runs some tests and gives you a red, yellow, or green light. Click the Help button next to a red or yellow light to get troubleshooting help from Apple's Web site. (Green means groovy.)

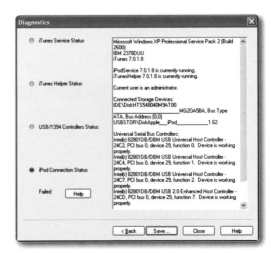

Updating Your iPod's Software

When iTunes 7 rolled into town, it brought with it a much less complicated way to update the iPod's own internal software—which Apple does occasionally to fix bugs and add features like the ability to play Store-bought games on older video iPods. No matter which iPod model you have, iTunes 7 and later handles the iPod updating without the need to download a separate installer program for the iPod.

If your iPod is formatted for Windows, update it on a Windows machine; likewise, update a Mac-formatted iPod on a Macintosh. You can tell which system your iPod is formatted for by choosing, on the iPod, Settings→About and scrolling down to the last line, which reads Format: Windows if you have a PC Pod. (If you've got a Mac-formatted iPod, you won't see anything.)

To make sure you have the latest version of the iPod's software, follow these steps:

❶ Have iTunes check for any updates. On a Mac, choose iTunes→Check for Updates. In Windows, choose Help→Check for Updates. This looks for both iTunes and iPod updates.

❷ Connect your iPod to the computer with its cable or dock. If your iPod is up to date, iTunes tells you so on the Summary screen and grays out the Update button.

❸ If iTunes finds new iPod software, you'll be prompted to download it. Click the Downloading icon in the Source pane to monitor your download's progress (shown below). Sometimes iTunes will have already downloaded the new iPod software. In that case, just click the Update button in the iTunes main window.

❹ Follow the instructions onscreen.

Older iPod models may require the use of an AC adapter to finish the update, but newer iPods mainly just sit there quietly with a progress bar and an Apple logo onscreen. Once all that goes away, your iPod screen returns to normal and iTunes displays a message box letting you know the update's complete.

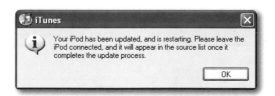

If you're updating your iPod Shuffle, play close attention to the progress bar on the iTunes screen and follow any instructions given. Since the Shuffle has no screen, iTunes is the place to look to see when the update process is done— usually by returning the Shuffle's icon to the Source list when it's good to go.

Starting Over: Restoring Your iPod's Software

Just like the operating system that runs your computer, your iPod has its own software that controls everything it can do. *Restoring* the iPod software isn't the same thing as updating it. Restoring is a much more drastic procedure, like reformatting the hard drive on your Mac or PC. For one thing, *restoring the software erases the iPod's hard drive (or flash memory, if you've got a Nano or Shuffle) entirely*.

So restore with caution, and do so only if you've tried all the other trouble-shooting measures covered in this chapter. If you've decided to take the plunge, first make sure you have the most recent version of iTunes (flip back a page for information on that), and then proceed as follows:

❶ Start iTunes, and connect your iPod to your computer with its cable.

❷ When the iPod appears in the iTunes Source list, click its icon to see the Summary information (in the main area of the iTunes window).

❸ In the Summary area, click the Restore button.

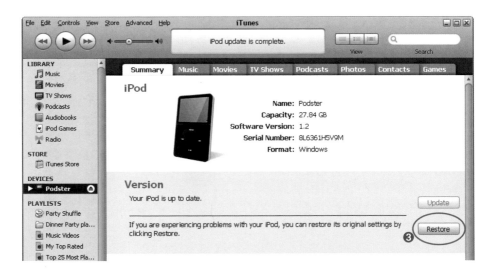

❹ Because restoring erases everything on your iPod, you get a warning message. If you're sure you want to continue, click Restore again.

❺ If you use a Mac, enter an administrator password and a progress bar appears on your iPod's screen. Leave the iPod connected to your computer to complete the restoration process. You may also see an Apple logo appear onscreen.

Tip If you manually manage your music and you restore the iPod's software, you'll lose any songs that are not already stored in your iTunes library. (For example, say you pulled some songs off another computer that you no longer have access to.) In that case you may want to get yourself a shareware program that lets you harvest your songs off the iPod (*www.ilounge.com* lists several).

After the restore process is finished, the iTunes Setup Assistant window appears asking you to name your iPod and choose your syncing preferences—just like when you connected your iPod for the first time. Let the iPod automatically update or add your songs, photos, and videos back manually and see if this little procedure has fixed the iPod's ailment.

Understanding the iPod's Battery Messages

Remember how you were taught that certain kinds of batteries (in laptops and camcorders, say) worked better if you occasionally fully drained and then recharged them? Forget it. You want to keep the iPod's lithium-ion battery charged *always*, or else you'll lose your clock, date, and other settings.

The color screen on the iPod and iPod Nano shows a green battery that depletes as you use the player. When the battery icon turns red, it's time to recharge. The screenless Shuffle communicates its battery needs through a small colored light: green for a good charge, amber for partially drained, and red for a battery that needs juice fast.

If you see a dull gray charging icon on your iPod's screen and the iPod won't turn on, the battery has run all the way down and the poor thing doesn't even have the energy to show its battery-charging color icon. Plug it into the computer, or an optional AC adapter, and give it about half an hour of power to get back to its regular screen graphic. When the battery gets this depleted, you may also have to charge it up for a while to even get the iPod to show up in iTunes.

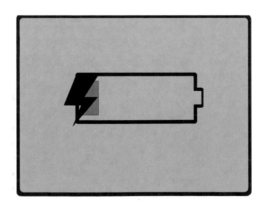

Apple's Tips for Longer iPod Battery Life

Apple has posted various recommendations on its Web site for treating the iPod battery to ensure a long life:

- Don't expose the iPod to extreme hot or cold temperature ranges. (In other words, don't leave it in a hot, parked car, and don't expect it to operate on Mt. Everest.)

- Take the iPod out of any heat-trapping cases or covers when you charge it.

- Put the iPod to sleep to conserve battery power. (Press the Play/Pause button until the iPod display goes blank and the iPod settles into slumber.)

- Even when you're not using the iPod, charge the battery every 14 to 28 days to keep it powered—even while it's sleeping. (It still needs power in sleep mode.)

- When you see the Low Battery icon or message, plug the iPod into the computer or an electrical outlet with the AC adapter. The iPod battery indicator shows roughly how much charge is left in the battery.

- Features like the backlight and the equalizer—or jumping around your library—can make the battery drain faster, as can using big uncompressed file formats like AIFF.

Replacing Your iPod's Battery

The iPod uses a rechargeable lithium-ion battery. Unlike players that run on a pack of Duracells, you can't easily pop out the old battery and replace it with a new one when it wears out after repeated charging and use cycles.

Which is not to say you *can't* replace the iPod's battery. It just takes a little more time and effort. If your battery is too pooped to power your Pod, here are some options:

- You get a full year warranty on your iPod battery (two years with the optional AppleCare protection plan). But Apple itself offers an out-of-warranty battery replacement service for $59 at *www.apple. com/support/ipod/service/battery*.

- Laptops For Less (*www.ipodbattery.com*), offers do-it-yourself iPod battery replacement kits for less than $20.

- OtherWorld Computing sells high-capacity NewerTech iPod batteries for all models of iPods. The company has instructional videos on their Web site, but will also replace the battery for you if you send them your iPod (*http://eshop.macsales.com/shop/ipod*).

- PDASmart.com will replace your iPod's ailing battery for $50 (parts and labor included) at *www.pdasmart.com/ipodpartscenter.htm*. The company can also fix broken screens and hard drives.

AppleCare—What It Is and Whether You Need It

You probably have an insurance policy on your house and car, so why not get one for your iPod? That's the logic behind getting the $59 AppleCare Protection Plan for your iPod.

When you buy a brand new iPod, you automatically get free telephone support to fix one problem within your first 90 days of iPod ownership, plus a yearlong warranty on the hardware. If the iPod starts acting weird or stops working altogether, Apple will fix it for free or send you a replacement Pod.

If you buy the AppleCare Protection Plan (available in many places where you buy iPods or at *www.apple.com/support/products/applecareipod.html*), you get:

- One full year of free telephone support from the date of your iPod purchase

- Two full years of hardware protection from the date of your iPod purchase

Your iPod's earphones, battery, and cables are all covered under the plan. If you need a repair or replacement, your iPod's covered. Paying an extra $59 to get the extended warranty may not appeal to everyone, but if you want a little peace of mind with your new iPod, it's a small price to pay.

Finding an iPod Repair Shop

If you're experiencing an iPod problem that's not listed or just won't go away, it may be time to visit the iPod Service Request page and fill out the form at *http://depot.info.apple.com/ipod*. Click the Continue link and, after you've scrolled down to the bottom of *that* page, fill in the form. You need to type in your iPod serial number and set up an Apple ID if you don't already have one. Then follow through with the Web forms for shipping and payment.

The iPodResQ Service is another option for the frantic. For $29, the company will send you a box to overnight your ailing player to the iPodResQ Repair Center, where they diagnose the problem and give you a repair estimate. If you accept the charge, they fix your iPod within 24 hours and pop it back to you by overnight mail. Call them at 1-877-POD-REPAIR, or go to *www.ipodresq.com* for more information.

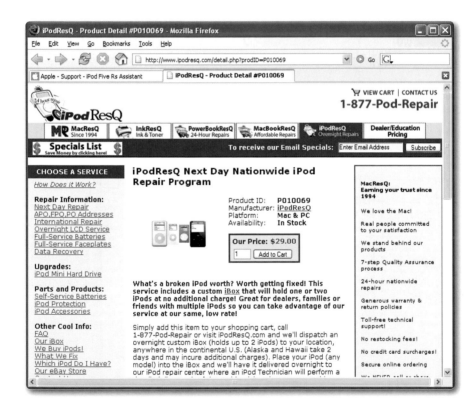

The TechRestore computer repair site has opened its own Pod Hospital as well and offers a range of fixes for broken screens, busted audio jacks, battery upgrades, and other ailments. You'll find more information at *http://ipod.techrestore.com*.

Where to Find Apple's iPod Tutorials, Demos, and Help

Apple keeps an online library of technical help articles on the Web, along with manuals and details about new iPod models and software updates.

• The iPod Service & Support page, which includes links to tips, tutorials, videos, a Frequently Asked Questions section, discussion forums, and top tech-support issues is at *www.apple.com/support/ipod/family*. Links along the right side of the page let you select articles appropriate for your specific iPod.

- The iTunes Service & Support page (*www.apple.com/support/itunes*) covers known issues with the program for both Windows and Macintosh systems. A crash course in using Apple's jukebox program is there, plus animated tutorials and How-To articles.

- For problems with billing, downloading, and computer authorization, the direct link to the iTunes Store Customer Service Center is *www.apple.com/support/itunes/store*.

 Computers and other electronic gear, including the iPod, contain toxic chemicals and other materials that can be harmful to the environment when dumped in landfills. If your iPod is dead for good with no hope of ever getting better, you can send it back to Apple and have it recycled in a way that pleases Mother Nature. Read more about Apple's recycling policy at *www.apple.com/environment/recycling*.

11

Advanced iPodding

Now that you've learned all the basics needed to have fun with iTunes and your iPod, you may be ready to move up a level on your path to iPod Guru. As you've seen, the iPod and iTunes experience lets you listen to your music the way *you* want to, but you don't have to stop there. Why not find cool new programs that let you do all sorts of *other* things with your iPod? Or find ways to broaden your playlist horizons? Or even make your own podcast?

This chapter kicks it up a notch and gives you some ideas of what else you can do with iTunes and the iPod besides just watching and listening.

Cool Software for Even More iPod Fun

There's something about the iPod that inspires creativity on many levels. Plenty of software developers have risen to the challenge of making programs that make the iPod even more useful. Once of the best resources is the iPod software area of the iLounge Web site at *www.ilounge.com/index.php/ipod-software*, where you can find all sorts of Podware.

Other spots around the Web you may want to check out include:

- **Talking Panda Software.**
  Want to learn how to speak traveler's French, teach yourself guitar chords, or store a reference library of 1,000 drink recipes—all on your iPod? Check out Talking Panda's stable of inexpensive iPod programs, specifically iLingo, iRocker, and iBar (*www.talkingpanda.com*).

- **iPod Directions.** This neighborly Web site uses Yahoo Local to download maps and driving instructions from Point A to Point B. Just add the downloaded files to your preferred Photos folder (Chapter 7) and let iTunes sync the images to your iPod; you'll never have to ask strangers for directions again (*www.ipod-directions.com*).

- **Doug's AppleScripts for iTunes.** Mac OS X folks who use AppleScript, Apple's built-in tool for automating certain tasks, will find more than 400 different scripts for managing iTunes and the iPod here (*www.dougscripts.com/itunes*).

Runners Alert: Use Your iPod Nano to Track Your Progress

Serious runners quickly discovered that digital audio players made the perfect buddies for that daily jog. Sure, you can listen to music on the run, but Apple and Nike have taken things further, letting runners turn their iPod Nanos into workout monitors to track time, distance covered, and calories burned as well.

You need a few specific things to make it all work:

- An iPod Nano

- A special pair of Nike+ running shoes

- The Nike+iPod Sport Kit

The Sport Kit, available for $29 at *http://store.apple.com*, comes with two electronic widgets: a wireless sensor that slips into a secret pocket in the special Nike+ shoe, and a small receiver that snaps into the dock-connector port on the bottom of the iPod Nano. Once you start running, the shoe sensor beams info from every step right up to the Nano, which displays the data on its screen and gives you audio feedback on your progress.

Later, when you're back at your computer and have synched up your Nano, all your workout info uploads to the *www.nikeplus.com* Web site, where you can track and chart your progress. For more information check out *www.apple.com/ipod/nike*.

Finding Alternative Headphones for Your iPod

Every new iPod comes with a pair of Apple-white earbud-style headphones, but not everybody loves them. If you're not a fan, you can swap them out with just about any pair of headphones that has a 3.5-inch stereo miniplug on the end. Here are a few models to consider:

- **Sennheiser PX 100W Supra Aural Folding Mini-Headphones.** Big sound for a not-so-big price, Sennheiser's collapsible over-the-ear headphones come in black or white and offer a great alternative to earbuds; around $40 on sites like *www.amazon.com*.

- **Blue Ant X5 Bluetooth stereo headphones.** Lose the uncomfortable earbuds and the wires, too, with these wireless, over-the-ear headphones. You need to attach the somewhat bulky Bluetooth audio streamer to the iPod to stream the music to the headphones, but then you can put the Pod in your backpack or leave it on the desk as you zone out to your tunes; $140 at *www.myblueant.com*.

- **Bose QuietComfort 3 Noise-Canceling Headphones.** These babies may be the Cadillac of headphones in both sound, fit, and price. The noise-canceling function can help you hear your iPod even over jet engines, street noise, and other sonic annoyances; $350 at *www.bose.com*.

Getting Ideas for Playlists

Chapter 4 explains how to make your own playlists, but if you're feeling uninspired, it helps to look around and see what other people are doing with their music mixes.

Obviously, the iMixes in the iTunes Store are a good place to start, and you have the added bonus of being able to buy all the songs on each person's playlist right there. The iTunes Essentials, iTunes Collections, and other themed song sets can also give you some ideas.

Other places to look for playlist inspiration include:

- **Fiql**, which bills itself as "the Playlist Sharing Community," has thousands of playlists made by members and sorted by genre, mood, or activity (*www.fiql.com*).

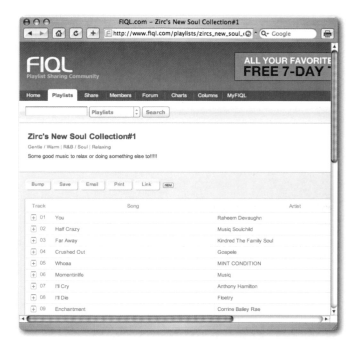

- **MusicMobs** lets its customers post their favorite playlists and tag them with keywords, (just like Flickr fans can do with their photos) for easy categorizing (*www.musicmobs.com*).

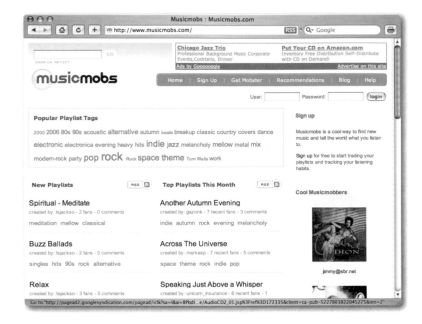

- **SmartPlaylists.com** is a site where people post their playlist creations as well as iTunes tips and other helpful info (*smartplaylists.com*).

What You Need to Make Your Own Podcast

Podcasts, as you may recall from Chapter 5, are radio-style audio shows. You can find thousands of them free in the iTunes Store. Podcasts can range from slick professionally recorded programs like the Pop Culture report from National Public Radio to a home-recorded dialog between two guys in a basement talking about the enduring appeal of *Star Wars*.

You don't need a fancy recording studio, a sound-mixing board, or pricey professional programs to make your own podcast. All you really need to make a podcast on your own computer is:

- A microphone

- Some inexpensive recording software

- An Internet connection

- Something to say

Poddcasting itself consists of two main activities: *recording* your show and *publishing* it to the Web—that is, making it available for anyone who wants to download and listen to it.

The Podcasting News site (*www.podcastingnews.com*) has a lengthy list of podcast-publishing programs and services for both Windows and Mac podjockeys. For the gung-ho podcaster, there's more information on using specialized podcasting software for Windows and Macintosh in this chapter, too.

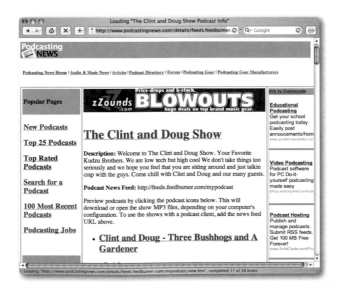

Recording Your Podcast

Once your computer's microphone is set up and you know what you want to say, it's time to record. If you don't have a recording program, you'll find tons of free/inexpensive audio software at shareware sites like *www.download.com* and *www.tucows.com*. n-Track Studio is one popular program.

If you have a Mac and a copy of iLife (with GarageBand 3 or later), you can get started by opening GarageBand and clicking the "New Podcast Episode" button on the main screen.

No matter what program you use to record yourself, here are some basic steps to follow:

❶ **Check the recording levels.** Experiment with your microphone's sound levels and adjust the volume settings so you sound clear and sonically undistorted.

❷ **Start talking.** Keep your mouth close to the microphone for consistent sound, and don't worry if you flub a word. You can always re-record the parts you messed up.

❸ **Edit and Save.** Most audio programs let you chop out boring parts, add background music, slip in sound effects, and so on to make your podcast sound as professional as possible. Save using the industry-standard MP3 format.

After you record your podcast, you have to put it somewhere where others can hear it. See the next page for details.

Publishing Your Podcast to Your Web Site or Blog

Once you've created an MP3 file of your podcast, you have to upload it to your Web site, blog, or wherever you want your listeners to find your audio file. You can post just a single MP3 file, but most podcasting gurus choose to embed their podcasts in an *RSS feed*. Doing so ensures that people with podcast-receiving or newsreader programs get notified automatically when any Web site they *subscribe* to (including yours) has new content available.

You can find many programs for Windows and Macintosh that automate the process of uploading your audio files all wrapped up in this nice RSS feed. For example, try Podifier (*www.podifier.com*) or FeedForAll (*www.feedforall.com*). Each program walks you through the steps for publishing your podcast and RSS feed to your Web site or blog.

Podcasting News has an illustrated tutorial showing how you can create your own RSS feed; you can find it directly at *www.podcastingnews.com/articles/Make_Podcast_Blogger.html*.

> **Tip** Got a microphone but no sound-in port on your computer? Do it the USB way with the $40 iMic from Griffin Technology (*www.griffintechnology.com*). The iMic works with both Windows and Macs. If you don't have the microphone either, consider the $40 MicFlex from MacMice (*www.macmice.com*), a flexible microphone that plugs right into the USB port.

Publishing your GarageBand Podcast to iWeb or the Web

GarageBand fans, listen up: Once you've perfected your podcast, save your finished file. Now you're ready to release your podcast onto the Web. If you have iLife '06 or later and a .Mac account, all you need to do is choose Share→ Send Podcast to iWeb. This bops the file over to your iWeb program, where you can upload it to your personal Web site.

If you don't have iWeb or a .Mac account, you can export your podcast and put it up on the Web site of your choosing. To do so, choose Share→Export Podcast to Disk; your podcast lands on your desktop. From there, send it to your Web site.

You can also export the podcast file into iTunes. Once you've saved your masterpiece in GarageBand, go to Share→Send Podcast to iTunes. GarageBand mixes the song and exports it as an AIFF file into a special iTunes playlist. By default, the playlist is named after whoever is logged on to the Mac, but you can change it in the GarageBand preferences.

Getting the iTunes Store to List
Your Podcast

Apple doesn't store podcast files on its iTunes Store servers, but the company freely invites podcasters everywhere to submit their shows for inclusion in its Podcast Directory. This listing then links back to your own server or Web site.

Keep in mind that podcasts in the iTunes Store need to meet certain technical requirements; Apple has the complete list of specifications posted at *www.apple.com/itunes/store/podcaststechspecs.html*, along with tutorials, sample feeds, and instructions on how to prepare your podcast files.

Once your podcast passes technical muster, all you need to do is hop into the Store, go to the Podcasts area from the link on the main page, and then click the big "Submit a Podcast" icon in the middle of the page.

Next, type in the link for your podcast's RSS feed and provide some basic information about your show so people poking around know what it's about. Your submission doesn't appear immediately after you complete the form; it may be reviewed before your show appears in the Podcast Directory.

 Note If your podcast contains any copyrighted audio material used without authorization and someone complains about it, Apple reserves the right to zap your show right out of its listings.

Where to Get the Latest iPod News

Keeping up with the ever-evolving world of the iPod can be a full-time job: What new models might be coming around the corner? What new accessories for the iPod are out there? How can I harvest the songs off my iPod since my hard drive croaked and I never, *ever*, backed it up?

If you find yourself on the lookout for iPod news, tips, and tricks, you'll find plenty of Web sites out there that aim to please. Here are some great ones to start with:

- **iLounge.** The most comprehensive iPod-centric site on the Web, iLounge concerns itself with "all things iPod, iTunes and beyond." News, tutorials, software downloads, user guides, in-depth product reviews, and discussion forums make this site a must-visit (*www.ilounge.com*).

- **iPodNN.** The iPod News Network rounds up the latest iPod-related headlines, product reviews, and more (*www.ipodnn.com*).

- **iPodRumors.**
  Sometimes more gossip than news, the iPod area of the feisty MacRumors site rounds up all the Podworthy buzz on the Web (*http://ipod.macrumors.com*).

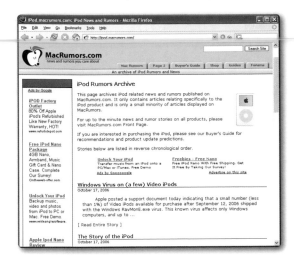

- **Topix.net.** A newsy site that collects stories from all around the Web, Topix also has a page just for news articles on your favorite music player (*www.topix.net/computers/ipod*).

Index

Symbols

5 Rs (troubleshooting) 200

A

AAC file format 53
About (Settings menu) 26
AC adapters 42, 205
accessories 195
 headphones 220
 Nike+iPod Sport Kit 219
accounts
 allowance 121
 Apple (iTunes Store) 105-107, 115
adapters, car stereo 186
address, billing (iTunes Store) 107
address book 164, 165
Add to Playlist command (iTunes) 88
Adobe Photoshop Album/Elements 152
AIFF file format 53, 209
AirPort Express 191, 192
alarm clock 31, 32
album covers. *See* artwork
album info., editing 67
albums, photo 154
allowance accounts (iTunes Store) 121
always on top option (iTunes mini-
  player) 49
Apple.com 200, 213
AppleCare Protection Plan 211

Apple ID 105
Apple Lossless file format 53
AppleScript downloads 218
artwork
 adding manually/automatically 68, 69
 Cover Flow view 54, 135
 custom 99
 downloading 110
 for movies/videos 135
 Grouped with Artwork view 54, 135
 printing for playlists 98, 99
 viewing on iPod 71
Audible.com 112
audio, recording 176, 177
audio books 26, 112
audio cable, connecting to home entertainment system with 189
authorizing/deauthorizing computers
  (iTunes Store) 126-128
Autofill (Shuffle) 78, 79
autosyncing 10
 Autofill (Shuffle) 78
 multiple computers and 76
 photos and 153-155
 playlists 89
 videos 136
 voice memos 177
auxiliary input (car stereo), playing iPod
  through 185
AVI file format 139

B

backing up files to
     CDs/DVDs **82, 96, 97, 148**
backlight timer **26, 37**
base station. *See* AirPort Express
battery
  car chargers **188**
  charging **13**
  charging **41, 42**
  icon **208**
  indicator **41**
  life **13, 209**
    backlight and **37**
    Hold switch and **20**
    iPod **2**
    Nano **4**
    Shuffle **5**
    sleep feature and **17, 33**
  replacing **210**
  sleep feature and **209**
  troubleshooting **208-210**
bell icon (alarm clock) **32**
Billboard charts **117**
billing address, changing
     (iTunes Store) **107**
books, audio **112**
Brick (game) **39**
brightness **26**
browsing your collection (iTunes) **54**
burning CDs/DVDs **82, 96, 97, 115, 148**
buttons (click wheel) **14**
  Menu **21**
buying music/videos/movies.
    See iTunes Store

C

calendar **25, 166, 167**
car charger **42**
car stereos, playing iPod through
  auxiliary input **185**
  cassette players **184**
  custom installation **186, 187**
  FM transmitters **182, 183**
  power sources **188**

car stereos, playing iPod
    through **180-188**
cases (iPod) **38**
cassette player, playing iPod
    through **184**
CDs
  backing up to **82**
  burning **115, 96, 97**
  diagnostics (Windows) **203**
  photos and **153**
  printing inserts **98, 99**
  ripping **9, 51-53**
celebrity playlists **117**
Change City option (clock) **31**
charging battery **13**
checkboxes, turning all on/off **52**
children's music (iTunes Store) **109**
cigarette lighter, as power source **188**
cleaning your iPod **38**
click wheel **14, 21**
  turning click sound on/off **27**
clock **25, 31-33**
  world clock **170**
collections (iTunes) **117**
columns
  adding/deleting (iTunes) **48**
  modifying/sorting (iTunes) **48**
  My Rating **57**
combination, setting
    (Screen Lock) **25, 36, 43**
compilations **27**
compression, sound quality and **53**
contacts **25, 27.** *See* address book
Contacts tab (iTunes) **75**
control ring (Shuffle) **5**
controls (iPod) **14-15, 21, 35**
converting files to different
    formats **60, 142-145**
copy protection **126**
copyright issues **27, 115**
  podcasts **227**
Cover Flow view (iTunes) **54, 135**
covers, album. *See* artwork

credit cards, updating info.
(iTunes Store) **107**
customizing menus **30**

D

data files, storing on iPod **172**
date and time **27, 31**
Daylight Savings Time (clock) **31**
deauthorizing computers
(iTunes Store) **128**
deleting
columns (iTunes) **48**
playlists **91**
demos **213**
diagnostics tools (Windows) **203**
dial-up Internet connections **108**
digital photos. *See* photos
directions (iPod Directions) **218**
disconnecting iPod from computer **12**
dock, connecting to home entertainment system with **190**
Dock connector **15**
Do Not Disconnect message **12**
downloading
dial-up connections and **108**
interrupted (iTunes Store) **123**
iTunes **202**
duplicate files, finding/deleting **64**
DVDs
backing up to **82**
burning **115, 96, 97, 148**
diagnostics (Windows) **203**
photos and **153**

E

earbuds. *See* headphones
editing
album info. **67**
iTunes Store account info. **107**
playlists **88**
song info. **66**
ejecting iPod from computer
(manually) **12**
entertainment systems. *See* home
entertainment systems

Equalizer (EQ) **26, 62**
essentials (iTunes) **117**
explicit material, parental controls and
(iTunes Store) **125**
external hard drive, storing music on **81**
extras, downloading **218**
Extras menu **25**
eyeball icon (iTunes Browser) **55**

F

Fast-forward/Next button **14, 35**
fast charge (battery) **13**
file formats **53, 152**
converting between **60**
for photos **152**
lyrics and **70**
sound quality and **53**
Thumb (.ithmb) **156**
video **139**
files
backing up **82, 148**
data, storing on iPod **172**
duplicate, finding/deleting **64**
finding in iTunes **55**
formats **53, 60, 70, 139, 152**
iTunes Library (storage system) **80**
manually managing **76, 77**
purchased, copying **129**
storage capacity **2, 4**
syncing. *See* syncing
text (notes) **174**
transferring between computers **126**
finding music already on computer **16**
five Rs (troubleshooting) **200**
FM transmitter, playing iPod
through **182, 183**
folders, organizing playlists in **95**
full charge (battery) **13**

G

games **25, 39**
buying **113**
Games tab (iTunes) **75**
Gapless Album option **67**
GarageBand, podcasts and **226**

gear icon (Smart Playlists) **94**
genre
finding music by (iTunes Store) **109**
Get Album Artwork command
(iTunes) **68**
Get Info box **134**
gift certificates/cards,
iTunes Store **118-120**
Google Video **140**
graphic equalizer (iTunes) **62**
Grouped with Artwork view **135**
Grouped with Artwork view (iTunes) **54**

H

hard drive
portable, iPod as **172**
hard drives
external, storing music on **81**
importing photos to iPod and **153**
storage capacity **2, 4**
Headphone jack **15**
headphones **220**
help **213**
Hold switch **15, 20**
home entertainment systems,
connecting iPod to **189-192**
with AirPort Express **191, 192**
home movies, converting for iPod **144**

I

iCal **166**
icons
battery **41, 208**
bell (alarm clock) **32**
blocking (parental controls) **125**
eyeball (iTunes Browser) **55**
gear (Smart Playlist) **94**
house (iTunes Store home page) **104**
playlist **93**
Radio (iTunes) **58**
safe (Screen Lock) **43**
twisty arrows (shuffle) **56**
white arrow (more info.) **104**
iLounge **218, 228**
iMixes **116**

iMovie HD **144**
importing CDs. *See* ripping CDs
installing iTunes **6**
Internet connection, dial-up **108**
Internet radio (iTunes) **58**
iPhoto **152**
iPod Nano. *See* Nano
iPod News Network (iPodNN) **228**
iPodRumors **229**
iPod Shuffle. *See* Shuffle
iTunes
account (iTunes Store) **105-107, 115**
adding artwork **68, 69**
adding videos to **134**
album info., editing **67**
always on top option (mini-player) **49**
buying music. *See* iTunes Store
converting video files with **145**
diagnostics tools (Windows) **203**
duplicate files, finding/deleting **64**
Equalizer **62**
files
backing up **82**
converting to different formats **60**
manually managing **76, 77**
finding music already on computer **8**
import settings, changing **53**
installing **6**
Internet radio **58**
iPod preferences, adjusting **74**
Library file (storage system) **80**
live updating (playlists) **94**
loading Shuffle **78, 79**
lyrics, viewing/adding **70**
Music folder, moving **81**
photos and **154**
playing videos **135**
rating songs **57**
reinstalling **202**
ripping CDs **9, 51-53**
searching library **55**
sharing music **59**
shuffling music **56**
song info., editing **66**
Sound Check (volume control) **61**
start/stop time, adjusting **65**
Store **9, 101, 130**

syncing 76, 95
  autosync 10, 78, 89
  manually 11, 79, 89, 91
  updating 202
  viewing iPod settings/contents 72, 73
  views 54
  Visualizer 50
  window, modifying 48, 49
iTunes Collections 117
iTunes Essentials 117
iTunes 45-83
iTunes Store 9
  account, setting up 105-107
  allowance accounts 121
  audio books 112
  authorizing/deauthorizing
     computers 126-128
  games 113
  gift certificates/cards 118-120
  interrupted downloads 123
  listing podcasts 227
  movies/videos 111
  navigating 104
  parental controls 125
  podcasts 114
  publishing playlists 116
  purchase history 130
  transferring purchased files 129
  usage rights 115
  wish lists 122
iTunes Store 101-130
iWeb, podcasts and 226

J

Just For You section (iTunes Store) 103

L

language setting 27-29
lap timer 168
Legal menu (Settings menu) 27
letterbox setting (videos) 138
library, photo 23, 157
Library file (iTunes) 80
list view (iTunes) 54
live updating (playlists) 94

locking iPod with password 25, 36, 43
lyrics
  viewing/adding in iTunes 70
  viewing on iPod 71

M

Main menu
  customizing 30
  settings 26
manually managing files 11
  artwork 69
  iPod Shuffle and 79
  photos and 153
  playlists 89, 91
  videos 136
manually managing files 76, 77
Menu button 21
menus 21-30
  customizing 30
  Extras 25
  Music 22
  navigating (click wheel) 14, 21
  Photo 23
  Settings 26
  Video 24
microphones (recording audio) 176
mini-player (iTunes), always on top option 49
MiniStore (iTunes Store) 102
movie posters. *See* artwork
movies. *See* videos
Movies tab (iTunes) 74
MP3 file format 53
  burning MP3 CDs 96, 97
  podcasts 225
MPEG file format 139
Multiple Item Information box 67
Music Cards, iTunes 120
Music folder (iTunes), moving 81
Music menu 22
Music Quiz 40
Music tab (iTunes) 74
music videos. *See* videos
My Rating column (iTunes) 57

N

naming
  playlists 86
  your iPod 10
Nano 4
  Nike+iPod Sport Kit 219
  storage capacity 4
network diagnostics 203
news (iPod related) 228
Next (Fast-forward) button 14, 35
Nike+iPod Sport Kit 219
notes feature 25, 174, 175
Now Playing option 28
NTSC broadcast standard (TV) 160

O

On-The-Go playlists 90
on/off control 20
optimizing photos 155, 156
Outlook
  address book and 164
  calendar and 166

P

PAL broadcast standard (TV) 160
Parachute (game) 40
parental controls (iTunes Store) 125
Party Shuffle 92
passwords
  locking iPod with 25, 36, 43
  parental controls (iTunes Store) 125
PayPal, using in iTunes Store 106
photos 151-161
  albums 154
  as CD covers 99
  CDs/DVDs and 153
  full-quality 156
  optimizing 155, 156
  Photos menu 23
  Photos tab (iTunes) 74
  putting on iPod 152-155
  slideshows 23, 158-161
  viewing on iPod 157
Photoshop Album/Elements 152
pictures. *See* photos

playing movies/videos
  controls 137
playing music/videos
  adjusting volume 36
  controls 14
  in iTunes 135
  Now Playing 28
  on car stereos 180-188
  on home entertainment
      systems 189-192
  on TV 146
  preferences 61
  scrubbing 35
  through portable speakers 193
playing music/videos 16-17, 137-138
playlists 221, 85-99
  adding songs to 88
  autosyncing and 89
  burning to CD/DVD 96, 97
  celebrity 117
  creating 86, 87, 90
  deleting 91
  icon 93
  iTunes Essentials 117
  live updating 94
  manual syncing and 89
  modifying 88
  naming 86
  On-The-Go 90
  organizing in folders 95
  Party Shuffle 92
  printing on CD inserts 98, 99
  publishing (iTunes Store) 116
  Purchased 124
  slideshows and 158
  Smart Playlists 93
  video 24
podcasts 24, 114, 223-227
  copyright issues 227
  listing in iTunes Store 227
  Podcast Directory (iTunes Store) 227
  recording/publishing 224-227
Podcasts tab (iTunes) 74
portable hard drive, iPod as 172
portable speakers 193
ports 15
power adapter 42

power sources (car stereo) 188
preferences
    adjusting with iTunes 74
    for dial-up connections 108
    language 27, 29
    playback
        Sound Check 27, 61
    Settings Menu 26
previews (iTunes Store) 104
Previous (Rewind) button 14, 35
programs, downloadable 218
Project Gutenberg 175
protecting your iPod (cases) 38
publishing playlists 116
publishing podcasts 225-227
purchased files
    copying 129
    Purchased playlist 124
    purchase history 130

Q

QuickTime 6, 139, 145

R

radio
    charts (iTunes Store) 117
    Internet (iTunes) 58
radios, car. *See* car stereos
ratings, parental controls and
        (iTunes Store) 125
rating songs 57
reading text files 174
recording/publishing podcasts 224-227
recording audio 176, 177
redeeming gift certificates
        (iTunes Store) 118
region setting (clock) 31
reinstalling iTunes 202
remote controls, docks and 190
removing gaps between songs 67
renaming files 66
repairs 212

repeat settings
    One/All (Settings menu) 26
    slideshows 23, 158
replacing battery 210
Reset All Settings command 27
resetting frozen iPods 201
resizing iTunes window 49
resolution, screen 3
restoring software 206
Rewind/Previous button 14, 35
ripping CDs 9, 51-53
    excluding songs 51
    import settings, changing 53
RSS feeds 225
running (Nike+iPod Sport Kit) 219

S

safe icon (Screen Lock) 43
Screen Lock 25, 43
screen resolution (iPod) 3
screen size (video/movie viewing) 135
scrolling (click wheel) 14, 21
scrubbing 35
Search (Music menu) 22
searching
    by genre (iTunes Store) 109
    iTunes library 22, 55
    iTunes Store 103
    on iPod 34
service requests (repairs) 212
session logs (stopwatch) 169
Set Combination. *See* Screen Lock
Settings menu 26
Setup Assistant 7
sharing music (iTunes) 59
Show in Playlist command 88
Shuffle 5, 78, 79
    Autofill feature 78
    battery indicator 41
    loading from iTunes 78, 79
    resetting 201
    storage capacity 5
    updating software 205
    USB port 7

shuffling
  music 26, 28, 56
    Party Shuffle 92
    skipping albums 67
    Smart Shuffle 56
  photos 23
sleep feature 17, 209
sleep timer 31, 33
slideshows 23, 158-161
  viewing on TV 160
Smart Playlists 93
Smart Shuffle 56
software 218
  restoring 206
  updates 202, 204
Solitaire 40
songs
  adding to playlists 86-88
  buying 110
  editing song/album info. 66
  searching for on iPod 34
  Show in Playlist command 88
  song lists, printing 98, 99
  stop/start time, adjusting 65
sorting columns (iTunes) 48
Sound Check (volume control) 27, 61
sound quality
  adjusting 62
  compression and 53
  voice memos 176
  volume, evening out
    (Sound Check) 61
sounds (click), turning on/off 27
Source panel (iTunes) 46
Sport Kit (Nano) 219
statistics (iPod) 73
stereos. *See* car stereos; home
    entertainment systems
stop/start time, adjusting 65
stopwatch 25, 168, 169
storage capacity 2
streaming Internet radio (iTunes) 58
submitting podcasts to iTunes
    Store 227
subscribing
  to periodicals 112
  to podcasts 114

Summary tab (iTunes) 74
support
  Apple.com 200
  AppleCare 211
  tutorials/demos/help 213
switches 15
syncing
  address book 164
  autosync 10, 76
    playlists 89
    Shuffle (Autofill) 78
  calendar 166
  manually 11, 76
    playlists 89, 91
    Shuffle 79
  photos and 153-155
  playlist folders and 95
  videos 136
  voice memos 177

T

Talking Panda Software 218
text files 174
time, setting 27, 31
timer 168, 169
TiVo, iPod and 141
Topix.net 229
trailers, movie (iTunes Store) 104
transferring purchased files between
    computers 126, 129
transitions (slideshows) 23, 158
troubleshooting 199-215
  5 Rs 200
  AppleCare 211
  battery 208-210
  diagnostics tools (Windows) 203
  reinstalling iTunes 202
  repairs 212
  resetting frozen iPods 201
  restoring software 206
  software updates (iPod) 204
  tutorials/demos/help 213
turning on/off 20
tutorials 213

TV
  broadcast standards 160
  Out/Signal 23, 147, 159-161
  shows
    buying 111
    recording on computer 143
    TV Shows tab (iTunes) 74
    Videos menu 24
  viewing
    pictures/slideshows 160
    videos 146

U

U2 Special Edition iPod 3
updating
  iPod software 204
  iTunes 202
updating, live (playlists) 94
usage rights 115
USB cable 7, 42
  disconnecting from computer 12
  Dock connector 15
  Do Not Disconnect message 12

V

Veoh 141
videos 133-148
  adding to iTunes 134
  burning to DVD 148
  buying (iTunes Store) 111
  compatible file formats 139
  converting for iPod 142-145
  finding online 140, 141
  movie trailers 104
  playing
    in iTunes 135
    on iPod 137
    on TV 146
  podcasts 24, 114
  transferring to iPod 136
  Videos menu 24
  widescreen settings 138

view options (iTunes) 54
Visualizer (iTunes) 50
voice memos 176, 177
volume
  adjusting 36
  evening out (Sound Check) 27, 61
  Volume Limit (Settings menu) 26, 36

W

warranty 211
widescreen setting (videos) 138
window, resizing (iTunes) 49
Windows file formats
  WAV (audio) 53
  WMV (video) 139
wireless base station.
        See AirPort Express
wish lists (iTunes Store) 122
world clock 170

Better than e-books

Buy *iPod: The Missing Manual*, 5th Edition, and access the digital edition FREE on Safari for 45 days.

Go to www.oreilly.com/go/safarienabled
and type in coupon code 7TH9-43LH-KX4W-3FHT-327K

Search thousands of top tech books

Download whole chapters

Cut and Paste code examples

Find answers fast

Search Safari! The premier electronic reference library for programmers and IT professionals.